The Jews of America

HISTORY AND SOURCES

The Jews of America

HISTORY AND SOURCES

FRANCES BUTWIN

Sources Edited by
ARTHUR C. BLECHER

BEHRMAN HOUSE, Inc.
Publishers   New York

ACKNOWLEDGMENTS

The illustrations are reproduced through the courtesy of: p. 6, Hispanic Society of America, New York; pp. 8, 10, 14, 28 (bottom), 31, 32, 34, 37, 38, 49, 50, 51, 57, 58, 59 (top), 64 (left), 73, 78, 81, 82, 83 (top right and bottom), 89, 93, 94 (top left), 96, 97 (top and bottom right), 98 (top), Independent Picture Service; p. 11, Bibliotheque Nationale, Service Photographie; p. 12, Museo Nacional del Prado, Madrid; pp. 16, 19, 21, 22, Jewish Publication Society of America; pp. 17, 20, 59 (bottom), 88, Library of Congress; p. 25, Chicago Historical Society, Photo by J. Sherwin Murphy; pp. 28 (top), 40, 41, 42, 43, 44, 72 (top left), 83 (top left), 92, 100, *Dictionary of American Portraits*, Dover Publications, Inc.; p. 36, California Palace of the Legion of Honor, Mildred Anna Williams Collection; p. 45, Hebrew Union College—Jewish Institute of Religion; pp. 52, 53, 54, 55, 56, *Jewish Daily Forward*; pp. 60, 76, Museum of the City of New York, Jacob A. Riis Collection; pp. 61, 62 (top), 67, New York Public Library; pp. 62 (bottom), 64 (right), 65, International Ladies Garment Workers' Union; pp. 63, 71, Museum of the City of New York, Byron Collection; p. 66, Simon and Schuster; p. 69, Harvard University Press; pp. 72 (top right), 84, Yivo Institute for Jewish Research; p. 72 (bottom), Warner Brothers; p. 74, Mandelstam Photo Service; p. 75, B. Manischewitz Company; p. 77, Community Service Society Archives; p. 79 (left), Detroit Tigers; p. 79 (right), Los Angeles Dodgers; p. 86, University of Pittsburgh; p. 87, Rutgers News Service, photo by Francis J. Higgins; p. 94 (top right and bottom right), United Artists Corporation; p. 94 (bottom left), Columbia Pictures; p. 97 (bottom left), National Broadcasting Company; p. 98 (bottom), New York Philharmonic; p. 99, Marlborough-Gerson Gallery, New York, Photo by Alice Rewald; p. 101, Mr. and Mrs. James Schramm, Burlington, Iowa; p. 102, Metro-Goldwyn-Mayer, Inc.; p. 103, D. J. Davies; p. 104, Viking Press, Photo by Jeff Lowenthal; p. 105, Israel Zamir; p. 106, New York Public Library, Astor, Lenox and Tilden Foundations.

I would like to express my appreciation to my friend, Mark Kiel, for his help and advice.   A.C.B.

This paperback edition published by

BEHRMAN HOUSE, Inc., 1261 Broadway, New York

10 9 8 7 6   85 84 83 82

International Copyright secured. Printed in U.S.A.

International Standard Book Number: 0-87441-062-2

Library of Congress Catalog Card Number: 73-2253

Contents

THE HISTORY

THE SOURCES

The History

Page from a Hebrew Bible. Toledo, Spain, 1491. A year later, Ferdinand and Isabella completed the Christian reconquest of Spain and expelled the Jews. From Spain the Jews went to the Near East, The Netherlands, and the Americas.

The Jews in Early America

1. *The Link with Columbus*

Though the first group of Jews to settle in the American colonies came to New Amsterdam in 1654, the history of the Jews in America begins with the discovery of America itself.

Christopher Columbus wrote in his diary: "After the Spanish monarchs had banished all the Jews from their kingdoms and territories, in the same month they gave me the order to undertake with sufficient men my voyage of discovery to the Indies." Was this mere coincidence, or was Columbus aware of a link between the banishment of the Jews and the order to undertake a voyage of discovery? We know that after Columbus had been turned down by the King of Portugal, he appealed to King Ferdinand and Queen Isabella of Spain for men, money, and ships, and that the Spanish monarchs for several years refused his request. Spain was not yet a sea power. The King and Queen, who by their marriage had united the provinces of Aragon and Castile in the north, were busy driving the Moors out of southern Spain, Christianizing their own people, and consolidating their kingdom. They had neither the time nor the money to risk on a venture such as Columbus proposed — to find a route east by sailing west.

But in the year 1492 two important events took place. In January, Granada, the last stronghold of the Moors in southern Spain, fell. At the end of March the King and Queen signed an order that all the Jews who wouldn't convert to Christianity leave within four months, and that their wealth and property be left to the Crown. At last Queen

Columbus at the court of Queen Isabella of Spain.

Isabella had the money—and the inclination—to listen to the sailor from Genoa. She conferred on him the title of Admiral and gave him three ships and 90 men for his voyage of discovery. Columbus sailed with the *Nina*, the *Pinta*, and the *Santa Maria*, on August 3, 1492, exactly one day after the final expulsion of the Jews from Spain.

2. *The Golden Age in Spain*

Among the 90 men who set out with Columbus were five Jews who had been converted to Christianity. The converts were officially called *conversos* or New Christians, but in popular speech they were known as *Marranos*. Two of the Marranos with Columbus, Bernal and Marco, were physicians, and a third, Luis de Torres, was his interpreter. Columbus sent the first reports of his discoveries to two of the Queen's ministers who had pleaded his cause and helped him with their own money—Luis Santangel and Gabriel Sanchez. These men were also Marranos.

Though many Marranos held high places at the Spanish Court and were as wealthy and proud as any Spanish grandee, their life was an uneasy one. The very word Marrano was a term of contempt. It meant "pig" in Spanish. Because the Marranos had been converted against their will, they still practiced their own religion in secret. They were under constant suspicion of heresy and often underwent questioning and torture. No wonder so many of them risked their lives and fortunes to follow the explorers to the New World.

8

To understand why some Jews were converted and why the majority who refused conversion—between 200,000 and 300,000—were expelled in 1492, we have to go back to what is known as the Golden Age of the Jews in Spain.

This Golden Age was a period of freedom, prosperity, and intellectual development for the Jews. It began with the conquest of southern Spain by the Moors in the eighth century and lasted into the fourteenth century—roughly about 600 years. The Moors, who came from North Africa, were an Arab people of the Moslem religion. They had developed a brilliant civilization, noted for its literature and art and the sciences of medicine, astronomy, and mathematics. They were tolerant toward the Jews, who had developed their own culture in Babylonia and North Africa. After the Moorish conquest of southern Spain in 711, great numbers of Jews flocked to Cordoba and other cities where they established their own communities and academies of learning. These academies produced religious as well as secular scholars, philosophers, poets, doctors, and linguists. Jewish scholars translated books from Hebrew, Greek, and Arabic into Latin, which later Christian scholars found useful. To this age belongs Moses Maimonides (1135-1204) who, like many great men, combined several fields of knowledge. He was a doctor of medicine, an astronomer, a Biblical scholar, and a philosopher. His most famous book, *A Guide for the Perplexed*, wove religion, philosophy, and the natural sciences into a harmonious whole, as a guide of conduct for enlightened man. His was a humanist concept of life far in advance of his day.

Trade flourished, too, as it usually does in an enlightened age when men exchange not only ideas but material goods. The Spanish cities made famous by the Moors, with the help of the Jews, still have a splendid ring in our ears—Cordoba, Malaga, Seville, Granada. The Moorish temples and palaces and Jewish synagogues, some of which later became Christian churches, had an influence on the architecture and art of Spain which persists to this day.

In the eleventh century the northern provinces of Spain united under Christian rulers and began to drive the Moors out of the Iberian Peninsula. In the savage wars that followed the Jews were caught

Moses Maimonides (1135-1204) left Cordoba at the age of 13, when fanatical Moslems—the Almohades—invaded the city. In about 1165 his family settled in Cairo where he later became physician in the court of the sultan Saladin. Maimonides's philosophical works have influenced both Jewish and Christian thought.

between two forces—that of Islam and Christianity. Some Jews went back to North Africa, among them Maimonides with his family. Others went to northern Spain where at first the Christian rulers welcomed them. Both Spain and Portugal were glad to utilize their skills in commerce and the sciences. Prince Henry the Navigator of Portugal employed the cartographer, Judah Cresques, who became known as "the map Jew," or the "compass Jew." Other Jews and Marranos compiled astronomical tables and invented the perpetual almanac, which proved of great use in the voyages of exploration.

But the Golden Age dimmed as the Catholic Church grew in power and began to overshadow the state. The Dominican Order, which controlled the Church in Spain, was more concerned with the conversion of non-believers than with the advancement of science. Jews who wouldn't accept conversion were threatened with loss of their property and positions in commerce, the government, and the army. Under pressure many converted. These were the New Christians, or in popular language, the Marranos.

But the act of baptism wasn't enough. The Church set up a tribunal, or court, which brought to trial any New Christians who were not zealous enough in following the new faith. This tribunal was called The Inquisition or Holy Office, with a Grand Inquisitor at its head.

It performed an elaborate ritual which culminated with torture to make the accused confess their "heresy." Thousands of victims were burned at the stake. The Spanish Inquisition sought out not only the Marranos, but people of other faiths, as well as Christians suspected of heresy. It followed its victims to the New World, and lasted in one form or another until almost the time of the French Revolution.

At the time of Columbus the Grand Inquisitor was Tomas de Torquemada, Queen Isabella's confessor, and it was he who prevailed upon the King and Queen to sign the order which in the words of Columbus, "banished all the Jews from their kingdoms and territories."

3. *The Sephardim and Ashkenazim*

The Jews who were driven from Spain, and soon after that from Portugal, fanned out over central and northern Europe, joining Jewish settlements which already existed or forming new ones. The country that proved most hospitable was Holland, which was to become a haven for religious and political dissenters of all kinds, including the English Puritans. The Netherlands was fighting for its own in-

A medieval Inquisition conducted by Dominicans. Two heretics (lower right) are about to be burned at the stake. The pope established the Inquisition in 1231, in order to weed out unbelievers. In 1478 Ferdinand and Isabella set up their own Inquisition to seek and punish converted Jews and Moors suspected of backsliding. The papacy had little control over the Spanish Inquisition and generally disapproved of it.

dependence from Spain, and perhaps for that reason welcomed exiles from that country. Besides, the Jews had skills and aptitudes that were useful to a nation which, like Holland, was trying to develop as a mercantile and colonial power. In Amsterdam there grew up a large and influential Jewish community which was to have some bearing on the settlement of the Jews in America.

Wherever the Jews from the Iberian Peninsula went they carried with them not only their religious heritage, but their Spanish and Portuguese language and culture. These Jews were called Sephardim, or Sephardic Jews, from the Hebrew name for Spain, *Sepharad*. They are distinguished from another branch of the Jewish people, the Ashkenazim, a word derived from the Hebrew name for Germany — *Ashkenaz*. These Jews had settled in Germany in the early Middle Ages and developed a German-Jewish culture and language. In time the term Ashkenazim, or Ashkenazic Jews, came to include also the Polish, Russian, and other East European Jews. All of them had the same religion, but the rituals differed somewhat. Then, too, the Sephardim considered themselves to be of an older and more patrician stock than the Ashkenazim and tended to keep themselves aloof. In America they were "the first settlers."

4. *New Amsterdam*

In September 1654, a French privateer, the *St. Charles*, tied up at a wharf in New Amsterdam at the tip of Manhattan Island. Aboard the *St. Charles* was a group of 23 Jews — men, women, and children — tired, bedraggled, and penniless but with plenty of spirit. They needed spirit, for the Governor of New Netherland refused them permission to land. Suppose he let them in, Peter Stuyvesant stormed, he would soon have to let in the papists, the Quakers, the Lutherans. Stuyvesant was known for his harsh, dictatorial methods and his strict adherence to the Dutch Reformed Church. In spite of the liberal policies of his employers, the Dutch West India Company, he kept tight control of his own little colony. His position was far from secure. His settlement was isolated in the New World, surrounded on all sides by the British, and by the Swedes in Delaware, with the only other Dutch settlement, Fort Orange, far up the Hudson River to the north. The Dutch had little agriculture. Their chief occupation was fur trading with the Indians.

How did the small band of Jews happen to come to this little Dutch outpost in North America, and where had they come from?

They were Sephardic Jews of Portuguese descent, but they had come from Recife (City of Reefs) in Brazil, a town now called Pernambuco. Brazil had been colonized by Portugal in the sixteenth century, and some Marranos had come there with the Portuguese explorers and settlers. Under Portuguese rule they could not practice their own religion. But when Holland captured some cities in Brazil and Guiana, the Marranos returned to their own faith. In 1621 the Dutch West India Company was formed in Amsterdam and some of the directors and stockholders were Jews. The Dutch took Recife in 1631 and among

13

The first group of Jews to settle in America came from
Brazil to New Amsterdam in 1654. Above, the city in 1670.

the shiploads of Dutch settlers were a number of Jews. They built a
synagogue and within 30 years had a community of 5,000 — more than
twice the number of Jews that came to the North American colonies
before the American Revolution.

When Recife was recaptured by the Portuguese in 1654, the Jews
were again set adrift. Many returned to Holland, some went to
Surinam (Dutch Guiana), others to Curacao, Jamaica, Barbados, and
other islands of the Caribbean. The little group on the *St. Charles*
headed north and reached New Amsterdam. They stayed on the ship
until the Dutch West India Company sent orders to Stuyvesant to let
them land. He submitted with bad grace, warning the newcomers that
they must not become a burden on the colony. They were allowed to
trade with the Indians on the Hudson and Delaware, but were not
granted full burghers' rights. Their leader, Asser Levy, protested
when the Jews were made to pay a tax instead of being allowed to
serve in the militia. Another leader of the group was Jacob Barsimson
who had come on a ship called the *Perebom* (Peartree).

One of the first rights the Jews asked for was permission to buy a
plot of land for a cemetery. This was a pattern to be repeated in each
new settlement. Long before they made plans for a house of worship,
the Jews wanted a piece of ground in which to bury their dead. As a
result the history of old settlers can often be traced not from buildings
which burn down or are demolished, but from sunken old gravestones.

Ten years later, in 1664, King Charles II of England sent his fleet
to capture New Amsterdam and claim the land for England. He re-
named the city New York, in honor of his brother, the Duke of York.
It seems appropriate that the first American town in which a group of

Jews settled came to have the largest Jewish population of any city in America, and indeed in the world.

5. *Newport, Rhode Island*

The second Jewish settlement in the American colonies was in Newport, Rhode Island. A small group of Jews came to Newport from Holland in 1658; others came later from South America, the West Indies, and from Lisbon, Portugal. By the time of the American Revolution, Newport had the largest Jewish community in America.

Jews came to the American colonies for the same reasons other colonists came — to seek political and religious freedom, and economic opportunity. Political rights, such as the right to vote, to hold office, and to serve in the militia, were granted to Jews only here and there in the colonies; in most places they were denied. Jews were considered "an alien nation," though they were not a nation at all, but came from many nations and spoke a number of languages. They had their religion in common and the practice of their religion was not denied to them. In New England, especially, where the Puritans studied the Old Testament and gave their children such Biblical names as Nathaniel, Ezra, Ezekiel, Abigail, and Rachel, the Jews were looked upon with respect. But the Puritans' theology had a strange twist to it. They believed in the Second Coming of Christ, when the dead would arise, a final judgment take place, and the millenium or new age would dawn. But they believed that before this Second Coming, the conversion of all the Jews would have to take place. The Puritans didn't try to force this conversion, but they awaited it with hope.

For a reading on
Israel
see page 147.

A few conversions took place. The American colonies, like the mother country, England, at first excluded Jews from colleges. (England did not grant degrees to Jews until 1871.) The first Jew to get a degree from Harvard was Judah Monis, who had come from Italy. He received an M.A. degree from Harvard in 1720, but it appears that before he could get a teaching post he had to become a Christian. In March 1722, in an impressive ceremony, Judah Monis was baptized at College Hall, Cambridge, and was appointed Instructor in Hebrew. He taught Hebrew at Harvard until 1760 and published *A Grammar of the Hebrew Tongue,* the first Hebrew grammar to be published in

America. Though he belonged to the First Church at Cambridge and left a bequest in his will to the widows of poor clergymen, Judah Monis stuck to one tenet of his old faith. He always observed the seventh day as his Sabbath.

A more liberal attitude was taken in 1769 by the founders of Rhode Island College at Providence (later Brown University). The trustees provided for complete freedom of religion for all students and exempted Jewish students from attending Christian services. The college received gifts of money from Jewish merchants as far away as Charlestown, South Carolina. Aaron Lopez of Newport donated 10,000 feet of lumber.

Rhode Island had been founded in 1636 by Roger Williams, a young minister who believed in freedom of religion for everybody. That was one reason why the Jews came to Newport. Another reason was that Newport was a prominent seaport and commercial center. The Sephardic Jews who settled there had business connections in London and Amsterdam and soon built up trade with other American seaports. Early maps of Newport show Bellevue Avenue lined with shops owned by Jewish merchants of Spanish and Portuguese descent. The shipowners and traders had such names as Rivera, Lopez, Mendez, and Seixas. The most prominent among them was Aaron Lopez who came from Lisbon in 1752 and became one of the "merchant princes" of his day. He and his brother Moses owned ships which carried cargos

For a reading on
Identity
see page 109.

For a reading on
Tsedakah
see page 122.

Aaron Lopez (1731-1782) settled in Newport in 1752. By 1776 he had a merchant fleet of 30 ships. When the British took Newport, Lopez moved to Leicester, Massachusetts. His commercial strength — and Newport's — was broken. He died in a carriage accident on his way back to Newport after the war.

Interior of the Touro synagogue, Newport, Rhode Island.

of goods to Europe and up and down the Atlantic coast. Letters from Charlestown merchants mention the exchange of such goods as rice, potatoes, "nutts," rum and molasses, and casks of red and white Lisbon wine. Jacob Rivera, in association with others, began to process spermaceti oil (whale oil) which was so important to American colonists in making candles and oil for lamps. By 1776 there were 1,200 Jews in Newport in a total population of 7,500.

Before they built a synagogue and appointed a rabbi, the Jews of Newport used to write to friends and relatives in Amsterdam and London for advice on religious matters in relation to births, marriages, deaths, and the observance of holidays. It took the letters so long to cross the ocean that they had to improvise their own rules. In 1763 the Jews of Newport built a synagogue which was designed in the Georgian style by Peter Harrison, an English architect. The Sephardic ritual was observed in this synagogue, which was named the Touro synagogue for its first officiating rabbi, Isaac Touro. It is the oldest synagogue in America still standing, and together with the Tuoro cemetery it has become a historic landmark of colonial America.

6. *Philadelphia*

The first Jews to appear in Pennsylvania came down from New Amsterdam to trade with the Indians along the Delaware River as early as 1655. "Israelites," as they were called, were considered a curiosity, on a par with the Indians. In fact, William Penn expressed the opinion, held by some colonists, that the American Indians were descended from the ten lost tribes of Israel. To the Jews who came to settle in his colony he granted religious freedom, but not full civil rights.

Early in the eighteenth century Lancaster, Pennsylvania, which was an important frontier post for the western fur trade, had a small Jewish community, with its own place of worship and a cemetery. In 1747 the Jews of Philadelphia held religious services in a rented room in Sterling Alley. Around that time there appeared an advertisement in Benjamin Franklin's *Pennsylvania Gazette* asking that sportsmen forebear from using the brick wall of the Jewish burying ground as a target for shooting practice. It further stated that anyone who reported these "sportsmen" would receive a reward of 20 shillings from the undersigned, Nathan Levy. This Nathan Levy, who had bought the burial plot, was a well-to-do merchant, a prominent citizen, and a member of Philadelphia society, who "played a very good violine" at a concert in the Music Hall of Philadelphia.

Not all the Jewish settlers in Pennsylvania owned burial plots or belonged to musical societies. Most of them were pack peddlers who went into the wilderness to barter with the Indians, exchanging a brass kettle, a gun, or a bottle of rum, for a bundle of deerskins. Others made a living as sutlers selling provisions to soldiers in the French and Indian wars. But the colonists who left records behind them in the form of business letters, newspaper notices, and wills must of necessity have been those who had business to transact by letter, wares to advertise in the papers, and money and silver plate to leave to their heirs.

One of the families that left such records was the Gratz family. Bernard Gratz was born in a town in Upper Silesia on the Polish-Prussian border in 1738, and left home as a young boy to seek his fortune in London. He arrived in Philadelphia in 1754. At first he worked as a clerk for another Philadelphia merchant, David Franks.

When he heard that his brother Michael was planning to come to America he wrote to him to bring from London about 20 silver watches, some "new-fashioned watch chains," 20 dozen women's shoes, and "a few dozen women's mittens in black worsted."

Within a few years the Gratz brothers were shipping to England cargos of raw furs, cattle, grain, and lumber, presumably in exchange for more silver watches and women's worsted mittens. This was the pattern of colonial trade—raw materials in exchange for manufactured goods. Soon England was imposing heavy duties on the export trade. In protest against the Stamp Act, which taxed all legal documents and ships' papers, the colonial merchants banded together to sign a non-importation agreement in Philadelphia in 1765, pledging themselves not to import goods from England until the Stamp Act was repealed. Among the signers of this agreement were Bernard and Michael Gratz.

The Jews of Philadelphia didn't start to plan a synagogue building until the 1770's. The synagogue was built on Cherry Street and dedicated in 1782 in the midst of the Revolutionary War. Its first rabbi was Gershom Mendez Seixas, who had been the rabbi of the New York congregation but had left at the time of the British occupation. This Cherry Street synagogue was used as a house of worship by Philadelphia Jews until 1825.

Michael Gratz (1740-1811) helped open up western lands for settlement and trade. With his brother Bernard he formed a land company with holdings in Ohio, Kentucky, Indiana, and Illinois. During the Revolution the Gratz brothers ran supplies through the British blockade.

An Exact Prospect of CHARLESTOWN, the Metropolis of the Province of SOUTH CAROLINA.

Charlestown, South Carolina, in the early eighteenth century. Founded in 1670, it became the greatest Southern seaport in colonial America.

7. Charlestown

The first Jew to be mentioned in South Carolina history was an interpreter, and he remains anonymous. When Governor John Archdale published *A New Description of that Fertile and Pleasant Province of Carolina* (London, 1707) he wrote of a remarkable incident that happened in 1695. Some Yammassee Indians "going a Hunting, about 200 miles to the Southward," had captured four Indians near St. Augustine, Florida, and brought them to Charles Town, intending to sell them as slaves in Barbados or Jamaica. After interviewing the captives, the governor set them free. The Florida Indians, wrote the governor, "could speak *Spanish* and I had a *Jew* for an interpreter." This Jew may have been a former Marrano.

Charles Town (now Charleston) was a busy seaport and the largest and most cosmopolitan city in the South. It drew many Jews of Spanish descent who came from England and from the British possessions in the West Indies. Such names as Simon Vallentine, Jacob Mendis, Abraham Avilah are mentioned in early documents. They are described as "merchants," a term which applied not only to those in the shipping trade but to peddlers and shopkeepers. South Carolina had a liberal constitution which in its original draft promised freedom of worship to "Jews, Heathens," and others. The final draft didn't mention the Jews, but they enjoyed most of the privileges granted to other dissenters, among whom were the French Huguenots.

The first Jewish congregation in Charlestown was organized about 1749. It was called *Beth Elohim*, the House of God, and its services were conducted in the Sephardic ritual. It moved from place to place until 1794 when a synagogue was built which General Lafayette on a visit to the city is supposed to have admired. It was destroyed by fire in 1835. The present *Beth Elohim*, one of the oldest reform synagogues in America, stands on a plot of land which had been donated to the congregation by the heirs of Joseph Tobias, who served as the president of the first congregation.

The cemetery of *Beth Elohim*, the first Jewish congregation in Charlestown. Graves in the cemetery date from 1762.

The *hazan* or cantor of that earliest congregation was Isaac Da Costa, a merchant who had come from London in about 1740. Da Costa is said to have "moved in the best Charlestown circles," belonging to the Masons and the Palmetto Society. He did business with Aaron and Moses Lopez of Newport and carried on an extensive correspondence with them. In Newport, Isaac Da Costa met the Congregationalist minister, Ezra Stiles, who made a point of meeting cultivated Jews and discussing the Scriptures with them.

To be Sold by Mſſrs *Carvallo* and *Gut-teres* at their Store in Broad-ſtreet, China taffeties, ſilk romalls, cherrydaries, ginghams, ſundry ſorts of Bengales, ſilk damasks, ſilk handkerchiefs, ſilk brocades, india perſians, broad cloths with linings and trimmings, duroys with ditto, ſhaloons, 3 fourth, ⁻ eighth and yard wide garlixs, platilloes, bag hollands, india and engliſh chints, ſeveral colours of cotton romals, callimancoes, white callicoes, mill'd and knitted caps, black durants, ſilk camlets with trimmings, mens & boys woofted & thread hose, flower'd fring'd & plain ribbons, flat & round ſilk laces, dyaper, table cloths & napkins of ditto, pins, ivorycombs, fine nuns thread, whited brown thread, brown oznabrigs, blue linnen, ruſſia linnen, 3 fourth linnen, checks, ſilk ſtays, bohea tea, mens & boys fine hats, mens, boys, womens & girls ſhoes, Boxes of Caftile ſoap, of dip't candles, & very good Limejuice, all at reaſonable rates, by whole ſale and retail.

A shopkeeper's advertisement in the South Carolina *Gazette*, 1735.

Another New England clergyman, Hezekiah Smith, came to Charlestown in 1769 to raise funds for Rhode Island College. He found an enthusiastic supporter in Moses Lindo, who had studied at the Merchant Taylor's School in London, but as a Jew, had not been officially registered or granted a diploma. Moses Lindo was a rare type of individual in colonial America. He was a technologist. His specialty was the processing of indigo dye from the plant of that name, which was grown in South Carolina and was, next to rice, the colony's largest item of export. Lindo had arrived in Charlestown on *The Charming Nancy* in 1756 as a representative of a group of London textile manufacturers who used great quantities of the royal blue dye. As an expert on indigo, or "indico," Moses Lindo did the selecting, appraising, and shipping. Later he was appointed by the governor "Surveyor and Inspector General of Indigo," an honorary title, since the only money he made was the commissions he received from the indigo planters.

The indigo expert had studied chemistry and he experimented with other vegetable dyes. One of them was a crimson dye which he extracted from a South Carolina berry. He wrote an article about it which was published in *The Philosophical Transactions* of the Royal Society in 1763. Moses Lindo died in 1764, shortly before the Revolution put an end to trade with Great Britain and ruined his beloved indigo industry. His modest estate was sold "at public outcry" in a back store on the Bay, where most of Charlestown's business was conducted.

8. *The Jews in the American Revolution*

At the time of the American Revolution there were about 2,500 Jews in the American colonies, though some sources put their number as high as 3,000, others as low as 1,500. The total population of the 13 colonies was about two and a half million. The Jews were a tiny minority, but a significant one. Their significance lay in the very fact that they were a minority. The words of the Declaration of Independence, "All men are created equal," held out a hope of freedom and equality to every group and individual, regardless of his creed or national origin. The Jews, who had been driven from so many places, and denied every human and legal right, saw in the successful outcome of the Revolution their chance to participate as free citizens in the building of a new nation. The Jewish minority was historically important as well. It was the nucleus of one of the largest and most varied immigrant groups to come to America in the nineteenth and twentieth centuries.

For a reading on
Family
see page 115.

Jews took part in the revolutionary struggle from the start. We have seen how the Jewish merchants, who were engaged in shipping and overseas trade, protested vigorously against the Navigation Acts and the Stamp Act. When fighting broke out, they continued to give support to the American cause. Early in the war the British captured Newport and the Jews of Newport chose to leave their homes and places of business rather than collaborate with the British. In general, the Jews were no different from other colonists, some of whom remained loyal to King George, while most joined the ranks of the revolutionists. Philadelphia became the gathering place for American patriots, and to Philadelphia came Jews from Newport, New York, Charlestown, and Savannah, Georgia. Americans liked to compare their struggle against tyranny to the ancient struggles of the Israelites. The Liberty Bell, which was cast 25 years before the Revolution, bears an inscription from the Old Testament, "Proclaim liberty throughout all the land unto all the inhabitants thereof" (Leviticus 25:10).

In their fight against Great Britain the colonists received help from France, partly because France was herself at war with England, but also because the ferment of the French Revolution was already at work. General Lafayette came from France to help the colonies, and the Polish generals, Kosciuszko and Pulaski, exiles from their own country, also fought in the Revolution. Jews from Europe were drawn into the fight as well. Benjamin Nones, born in Bordeaux, France, came to Philadelphia in 1777 and enlisted in Captain Verdier's regiment under General Pulaski. He fought in all the battles of the Carolinas and at the siege of Savannah. He became a colonel at the head of 400 men, many of whom were Jews. At the battle of Camden, South Carolina, General de Kalb, a professional soldier who had come with Lafayette, was critically wounded and it is said that Nones helped carry him from the field of battle. After the war Benjamin Nones went to Philadelphia where he became an official interpreter of French and Spanish for the new government. Nones was an ardent supporter of Thomas Jefferson and when he was attacked in the newspapers he replied, "I am a Jew . . . and for that reason am I a republican. In republics we have rights, in monarchies we live but to experience wrongs."

Francis Salvador owned an indigo plantation in the northwestern part of South Carolina. He came from London in 1773 and soon became associated with other Carolina planters and was elected to the Provincial Congress from his district. He has the distinction to have been the first Jew elected to a popular assembly, because this provincial congress became the first Assembly of the State of South Carolina after independence was declared. When the British fleet attacked Charlestown he joined the state militia and became an officer. His regiment had to defend "the back country" which was being overrun by Tories and hostile Indian tribes. On August 1, 1776, his regiment was ambushed by the Indians. He was shot down from his horse and then scalped. He died so early in the Revolution that his name appears only in South Carolina history. A plaque dedicated to his memory in Charleston reads:

> Born an aristocrat, he became a democrat,
> An Englishman, he cast his lot with America;
> True to his ancient faith, he gave his life
> For new hopes of human liberty and understanding.

Mordecai Sheftall was a native of Savannah, Georgia. He was a prosperous merchant and according to the British, "a very great rebel." He became chairman of the Rebel Committee of Christ Church Parish (Savannah) and Commissary General of Purchases and Issues. It was his task to purchase food and supplies for the fighting forces and he was so meticulous in the discharge of his duties that he left

Robert Morris, George Washington, and **Haym Salomon** stand in Heald Square, Chicago. *(Courtesy Chicago Historical Society)*

numerous letters, accounts, and receipts behind, which are a good source for the student of the day-to-day events of the war in the South. When Savannah fell, he was captured by the British, put on a prison ship with his son, and taken to the West Indies. He underwent quizzing by the British, and suffered many humiliations both as a Jew and a rebel. After the war he received a grant of land from the American government in recognition of his services.

There is a monument in Chicago (erected in 1941) which has three figures — George Washington in the center, on one side Robert Morris, and on the other Haym Salomon. Robert Morris was the Superintendent of Finance during the Revolution. Since Congress had no power to impose taxes, raising money to pay, feed, and clothe the army was a formidable task. Loans came from France and Spain, but these were in the form of notes which had to be cashed or "discounted." Haym Salomon was the broker who discounted these notes. More than that, he made personal loans to Jefferson, Randolph, Madison, and other delegates to the Continental Congress. James Madison, who was to become the fourth President of the United States, wrote to his friend Edmund Randolph that he was resorting to loans from Salomon, "with great mortification," because "he obstinately rejects all recompense...To a necessitous delegate he gratuitously spares a supply out of his private stock."

25

Who was Haym Salomon? He was born in Lissa (Leszno), Poland, left home as a boy, traveled all over Europe, learned many languages, and acquired a thorough knowledge of banking and finance. After the partition of Poland in 1772 he went to London, and two years later came to New York. He became associated with American patriots, was arrested by the British as a spy and condemned to death. Somehow he escaped and went to Philadelphia where he advertised himself as a broker and then offered his services to Robert Morris. He was a practical man who helped the American cause in practical ways. That he did it generously without much gain to himself shows that he was also an idealist. He donated a large sum of money to the building of the Philadelphia synagogue in 1782, and later sent money through Amsterdam business agents to his needy parents in Poland. Though he had handled huge sums for the American government, at his death he left very little to his family.

At the end of the Revolution each of the 13 states had its own constitution and its own set of laws. Some states had outlawed slavery. Some had religious restrictions on voting and holding office. These were enforced in indirect ways. For instance, before accepting office, a person had to swear a Christian oath, which a Jew couldn't do. Thomas Jefferson, then governor of Virginia, opposed such restrictions. In 1786 the state of Virginia, under Jefferson's influence, passed the Statute of Religious Liberty, which gave equal civil rights to people of all religions. Soon the other states followed Virginia's example. By the time the new nation was established it was the only nation in the world which granted the Jews economic, religious, and political equality with other citizens.

For a reading on *Integration* see page 135.

The Jews from Germany and Central Europe: 1820-1880

1. *Medieval Myth*

In 1820 Sir Walter Scott, the English poet and novelist, published *Ivanhoe,* a romantic novel about the Crusades, set in twelfth century England. One of the heroines in *Ivanhoe* was the beautiful and spirited Rebecca, daughter of Isaac, the Jew, a miser who was torn between love for his daughter and his money. Scott modeled his heroine after Rebecca Gratz about whom he had heard from his American friend, Washington Irving. Irving, the author of "The Legend of Sleepy Hollow" and "Rip Van Winkle," had met Rebecca Gratz at the home of his fiancée in Philadelphia. Born in 1781, the daughter of the well-to-do merchant, Michael Gratz, she was a charming and cultivated young woman who moved in the best social circles. In later life she became devoted to good works and founded a home for orphans and the first Hebrew Sunday School Society in 1838. It seems odd that Sir Walter Scott had to go so far afield to find a model for the exotic Rebecca over whom knights fought in tournaments. In describing her and her miserly father he was, in fact, following a literary convention which was founded on myth.

Until well into the nineteenth century few Christians in Europe mingled with Jews on an equal footing. There had been Jewish communities in medieval Europe, not only in Spain, but in Italy, France, the Rhineland, and Bohemia. But the Jews were excluded from feudal society. They were not lords or vassals. They could not hold land and work on it. They were considered the king's chattels and he could do with them as he pleased. If he found them useful, they stayed; if not, he expelled them. Some Jews found places at Court as the king's personal physicians, more often as moneylenders and treasurers who provided the money the king needed to fight his wars. In return the

Rebecca Gratz (1781-1869) of Philadelphia. Sir Walter Scott drew upon Washington Irving's description of Rebecca when he wrote *Ivanhoe*, published in 1820.

king gave the Jew his protection, sometimes his friendship. A king or a feudal baron might boast of his clever and resourceful "Court Jew" as he might boast of his court jester or troubador.

Jews who lived in towns and were craftsmen, such as goldsmiths, weavers, tailors, or shoemakers, were not admitted to the Christian guilds. If they were merchants they had to pay heavy taxes for the privilege of doing trade Indeed, they had to pay taxes simply for permission to live in the town. They were not allowed burghers' rights, couldn't hold office or mingle freely with the other townspeople. But as long as they could work they managed to get along and sometimes to prosper.

Susskind von Trimberg (right), a German troubadour of the thirteenth century. His conical hat marked him a Jew.

On the continent and in England the feudal serfs, who were tied to the land and oppressed by the nobles, looked upon the Jews with hatred and suspicion. The Jews seemed to have more freedom than they. They were learned—they knew how to read and write and often spoke more than one language. Above all, they knew the language of numbers. They could do sums and handle coins with ease. Besides, the Jews practiced a different religion from their neighbors, followed strange customs, observed their own holidays, ate different foods. Weird tales began to be circulated about these mysterious people. They were devils in disguise, they had tails like monkeys, hidden under their long gaberdines, they used Christian children's blood in their rites, they practiced witchcraft. The clergy and nobles found it to their advantage to encourage these tales. If a peasant lost his bit of land, if the crop failed, or a child died of the plague, someone had to be blamed. It was easy to lay the blame on the Jew. And so a myth grew up of the diabolical, miserly Jew who owned treasures that everyone coveted. One of his treasures was gold; the other a beautiful daughter. Two hundred years before Sir Walter Scott wrote *Ivanhoe*, Shakespeare had drawn on this myth when he created the beautiful Jessica and her miserly father, Shylock, in *The Merchant of Venice*.

For a reading on *Anti-Semitism* see page 140.

2. *The Ghetto*

There were not many Jews in England until modern times. They had come from France with William the Conqueror in 1066, were expelled in 1290, and not allowed to return until Oliver Cromwell gave them permission to do so in 1656. For two centuries Jewish life in England followed a pattern like that of medieval Europe. The Plantagenet kings borrowed money from them to fight the barons. A wealthy Jew, Aaron of Lincoln, even loaned money for the building of abbeys and of Lincoln Cathedral.

Lending money at interest was denounced by the Church as usury, and so this despised calling was shifted onto the Jews, even though the Jewish religion also forbade usury. The law required that the money-lenders accept "pledges" from the borrowers. When the borrowers couldn't redeem these pledges the Jews were accused of avarice and greed. They accumulated some wealth in the form of armor, jewels, houses, even costly church plate. But the kings and barons generally managed to get it back in the form of taxes, or simply by seizing it. In time even money-lending was forbidden to the Jews and they became wretchedly poor. They crowded into the towns in special quarters assigned to them and followed humble occupations. Threadneedle Street in London, on which a handsome synagogue once stood, gives a clue to one occupation they followed.

Nearly every city in Europe had its Jewish quarter. In Imperial Rome it had been called by a Latin name—*Vicus Judaeorum.* In Spain it became *Judaria,* in France *Juiverie,* in Germany *Judengasse,* in Austria and Bohemia *Judenstadt.* Often these quarters grew up naturally near a Hebrew academy, a busy marketplace, or a synagogue. Living close together the Jews felt safer from outside attack.

For a reading on **Community** *see page 112.*

In the sixteenth century these Jewish quarters became known as ghettos. No one is sure about the origin of the word *ghetto,* but the most commonly held theory is that it came from the word *giotto,* a cannon foundry near which the Jewish quarter in Venice was located. It was about this time that the ghettos lost their voluntary character and became compulsory. In 1556 Pope Paul IV established the first compulsory ghetto in Rome on the left bank of the Tiber. The Roman ghetto was enclosed by a high wall and had a gate which was locked from sundown to sunrise, as well as on Sundays and Christian holidays. The Jews were not allowed to live anywhere else in the city. It became a model for such ghettos in the rest of Europe.

The rules varied from place to place. The Jews were made to wear a yellow badge, a peaked hat, a long gaberdine, or some other distinctive garment. In Rome they had to march in a procession once a year carrying their *Torahs,* or Scrolls, and beg permission of the Pope to allow them to remain another year. In most places they paid a heavy tax. If they were allowed to trade outside the ghetto walls, this trade was hedged in by various rules. For instance, they might sell used clothing (but not new garments), old jewelry, and second-hand goods of all kinds. This gave the Jewish merchants a shabby, transient character and turned most of them into old clothes and junk dealers. Going through the marketplace with their yellow badges, carrying their stock of goods in and out of the ghetto wall, they were often jeered and insulted by the populace.

The ghetto in Frankfurt, Germany, early nineteenth century.

Because certain areas were designated for the ghettos they soon became overcrowded. New stories had to be added on top of old houses. The streets were narrow and gloomy, often dirty. Little sunlight and air penetrated the densely built up areas. When the compulsory ghettos were finally abolished, the term *ghetto* continued to be applied to any poor and crowded neighborhood occupied by Jews, and later by other segregated minority groups.

Life in the European ghettos was not always mean and squalid. In Frankfurt-am-Main, Trieste, and Prague the ghettos were cities-within-cities. Mayer Amschel Rothschild (1743-1812), the founder of the Rothschild banking family, had an impressive house in the Frankfurt ghetto. The Prague ghetto was famous for its Talmudic academies to which Hebrew scholars flocked from all over Europe. The Jews of Prague had an autonomous government, with a chief rabbi, a council of elders, and their own courts of law. They had their own town hall, and four craft guilds, of goldsmiths, tailors, butchers, and shoemakers. Holidays were celebrated with pageantry. There were feasts and processions, and once a year a kind of carnival called *Purimspiel* during which troupes of players put on masks and costumes and enacted the *Spiel* or play about Queen Esther and Haman. At one time the religious leaders in the ghetto became alarmed at all the display and began exhorting their people to pay less attention to feasting and fine clothing, and more to prayers and acts of piety, just as the prophets of old had exhorted the people of Palestine.

For a reading on
Community
see page 112.

In medieval France, bands of armed men attacked the
Jews in their homes and synagogues. The massacres were
often led by Crusaders on their way to chase the Turks
out of the Holy Land.

Even while the ghettos were becoming a way of life for the Jews
of western Europe, certain forces began driving them out. The
Crusades were one such force. Armed bands who gathered to march
against the Saracens in the Holy Land first turned on the "infidels" at
home. With the cry of "Death to the Christ-killers!" fanatical mobs
roamed the cities, looted and burned Jewish homes and synagogues,
tortured and killed those who tried to defend themselves. Rather than
give up their faith or submit to torture, thousands of Jews chose to
die by their own hand. Mothers killed their children, then leaped into
the Rhine and drowned. Young men tried to resist and died. Elderly
men marched in processions carrying their sacred scrolls and chanting
"Shema Isroel," "Hear O Israel," as they went to their death.

Another force was the Black Death, or Plague, which ravaged
Europe in the twelfth and thirteenth centuries. In their ignorance of
what caused the Plague, the people blamed the Jews for casting evil
spells and poisoning the wells and rivers. They believed that if the
Jews were driven out, the Plague would go. Driven from western
Europe and Germany by the Crusades and the Black Death, and by
wars such as the Hussite War in Bohemia, the Jews began to look
about for new places of refuge.

3. *Poland*

To the east of Germany in wide, fertile fields and plains, and
among deep forests lived a Slavic people who had been pagans until
they came under the influence of the Roman Church in the tenth
century. Between the tenth and thirteenth centuries, they accepted

Christianity, fought off several Tatar invasions, and formed the kingdom of Poland. Poland was an agricultural country made up of large estates owned by nobles, or *pans*, and cultivated by peasants. A middle class was needed to build up the towns and develop trade with the West. For this purpose the Polish kings began to import German traders and craftsmen. In 1264 King Boleslav invited the Jews from Germany to settle in Poland. As an inducement he issued a charter which gave the Jews freedom to travel, offered protection from attack, and declared the slanders against them to be false. More Jews came to Poland when Casimir the Great (1330-1370) gave them the right to buy or rent land anywhere in the kingdom.

Poland extended its boundaries to Lithuania and the provinces on the Baltic Sea, as well as to Galicia and the Ukraine on the Rumanian border. Under the benign rule of the Polish kings Jews settled in every corner of the land, and established in the towns and villages communities called *kahals*. These kahals built schools and synagogues, and set up courts of law and societies for the care of the sick and poor. The Jewish craftsmen organized their own guilds. Jews leased and administered salt mines, became agents and overseers on the estates of the *pans*, and collected taxes from the peasants.

For a reading on *Tsedakah* see page 122.

The Ukraine had once belonged to the Cossacks, a proud and warlike people, who had more in common with the Tatars than with the Poles. They resented the rule of the Polish nobles and clergy. Poland was Roman Catholic, and the Cossacks were of the Greek Orthodox faith. Their church was taxed, and the tax collector was often a Jew, who had the keys to the church and wouldn't open it until the tax was paid. Oppressed by the Polish nobility, the Cossacks came to hate and resent their agents, the Jews.

This resentment flared up in the Cossack uprising of 1648. Led by their Hetman (headman) Bogdan Chmielnicki, who had been trained in wars against Turkey, the Cossack horsemen overran the Ukraine and the nearby provinces of Podolia and Volhynia. In rebellion against the Poles, they also vented their hatred against the Jews. They stormed into synagogues, slashed the holy arks, trampled on the scrolls, and set fire to the wooden structures. They mutilated, tortured, and killed the inhabitants of whole villages.

When **Bogdan Chmielnicki (1595-1657)** led the Cossacks of the Ukraine in an uprising against Polish rule, his men killed thousands of Jews. Chmielnicki put the Ukraine under Russian protection in 1654. Ten years after his death Russia and Poland divided the Ukraine between them.

The Cossacks rode west and besieged Lwow (Lemberg), demanding that the city council surrender the Jews. When the town council refused, they asked for a ransom and after collecting the ransom, killed the Jews anyway. The Cossack wars lasted off and on for seven years. During that time between 300,000 and 400,000 Jews died, were driven out, or were sold into slavery to the Turks. The Chmielnicki massacres have been called the greatest disasters the Jews suffered until the time of Hitler.

One of the towns of the Ukraine that lay in the path of the Cossacks was Pereyeslav, which 200 years later became the birthplace of the Jewish writer, Sholom Aleichem. Sholom Aleichem wrote with humor and sympathy of the people who lived in the little towns and hamlets of the Ukraine. In a story called "The Town of the Little People," he described a town which he called Kasrilevka and spoke of its old cemetery, rich in graves, which "They [the Jews] still value as they might a treasure, a rare gem, a piece of wealth.... For this is... the place where their ancestors lie, rabbis, men of piety, learned ones, scholars and famous people, including the dead from the ancient massacres of Chmielnicki's time..." Two hundred years after the event these "massacres of Chmielnicki's time" had become part of folk legend.

The Jews of Poland who survived the Cossack massacres never regained the privileges they had enjoyed under the early Polish kings. Poland itself became involved in foreign wars and in civil strife and lost much of its territory and prestige in Europe. Outbreaks against the Jews became common. Frightened and bewildered by the hostility of the people around them, the Jews shrank more and more from contact with the outside world. As often happens with a persecuted people, they fell prey to strange superstitions, began to believe in omens and evil spirits, and welcomed many self-appointed "messiahs" and miracle workers.

For a reading on
Anti-Semitism
see page 140.

Early in the eighteenth century a man appeared who called himself Baal Shem Tov — Master of the Good Name. He founded a movement called Hasidism, which emphasized joy rather than gloom, kind deeds rather than formal piety. It did some good by revitalizing religious beliefs and making the hard lot of the people more bearable, but it set its adherents even farther apart from the outside world. By "outside world" we mean western Europe toward which some Jews were beginning to return.

4. *Return to the West — Fall of the Ghettos*

The Chmielnicki uprisings in Poland coincided in western Europe with the end of the Thirty Years' War (1648). This had been mainly a religious war and when it was over, both Catholic and Protestant countries turned to rebuilding their ruined economies. With the passing of the feudal system, the religious persecutions of the Middle Ages had disappeared. The people in general became less superstitious and bigoted in their outlook. The emphasis on economic development and the rational spirit of the age favored the Jews. The descendants of those who had once fled eastward began to return to western Europe.

Holland which had received the Sephardic Jews earlier in the century now began to admit Ashkenazim from eastern Germany and Poland. Amsterdam became famous for its Jewish scholars, philosophers, and scientists, for its shipping merchants and craftsmen in gold and silver and precious stones. The Dutch masters used Biblical subjects in their paintings as well as scenes from contemporary Jewish life and portraits of notable Jews.

A group of Amsterdam merchants petitioned Oliver Cromwell, the Lord Protector of England, to lift the ban on the Jews. He complied not only for humanitarian but for practical reasons. The Jewish directors of the East India Company had international contacts and he needed their services. We have noted earlier that some of the Sephardic Jews of England came to settle in America.

35

Portrait of a Rabbi by Rembrandt van Rijn (1606-1669). Rembrandt lived for many years in the Jewish quarter of Amsterdam. Among the Jews he found models for some of his finest portraits as well as for drawings and etchings of Biblical subjects.

Germany was still divided into a number of states. Frederick the Great of Prussia (1712-1786) singled out certain Jews for favor and gave them special privileges such as the right to travel and to live in certain cities, like Berlin. These "favored" Jews helped to make Germany a great industrial nation by building textile factories, railroads, and later electric plants. Many distinguished themselves by their scholarship. Moses Mendelssohn, who had been born of a poor family in Dessau, came to Berlin and became the founder of the Jewish movement called the *Haskalah* or Enlightenment. He translated the five books of Moses into German with a parallel text in Hebrew. From this text of the Bible the Jews learned the German language.

Most of the German Jews still lived in ghettos. In the border province of Alsace-Lorraine they worked as peddlers and moneylenders. Strasbourg, the capital of Alsace, admitted these peddlers only during the day. In the evening a loud blast from a trumpet drove them back to their ghetto-slums in outlying villages. Other towns in the Rhineland imposed on the Jews special taxes and limited their places of residence and occupations.

At the same time during the eighteenth century, philosophers in England and France were spreading the new doctrine of the rights of man. There were oppressed people everywhere, peasants and townspeople without legal rights, often without work. Economically these people were even worse off than the Jews. These were the people who answered the call of the French Revolution, stormed the Bastille, and overthrew the French monarchy. It was the French Revolution and the events that followed it which finally overthrew the Jewish ghettos.

In 1791 the French Assembly granted equal rights to the Jews of France. After the French Revolution Napoleon was hailed as a liberator by many small countries and minority groups which had been under German or Austrian rule. His troops marched into the Rhineland and Italy, and wherever French soldiers marched in, they battered down the walls of the ghettos. As the ancient walls crumbled, martial bands played, fireworks were set off, and people cheered and embraced each other — both Jews and their Christian neighbors.

The breaking down of the ghetto walls had a double result. It brought thousands of Jews, especially in France, into contact with the outside world, and gave them a chance to enter trades and professions. At the same time it did away with some of their old privileges of autonomy and self-rule. The Jews were now guided not by their rabbis and elders, but by the law of the land. For instance, one of the rights granted by the French Assembly was the right to civil marriage. French Jews became Frenchmen first, and Jews only in respect to their religion. Later this happened in Germany as well. The German Jews considered themselves to be Germans "of Hebraic or Mosaic persuasion."

Synagogue of the Portuguese Jews in Amsterdam, dedicated in 1674.

The *Judengasse* or Jewish quarter
of Vienna. Late nineteenth century.

5. *The Jews from Germany*

Between 1820 and 1870 the population of the United States increased from 10 million to 40 million. Most of this growth was due to the great waves of immigration from central Europe, and especially from Germany. Because the census listed the immigrants by the country they came from, such as Germany, Austria, or Bohemia, it is hard to determine just how many of the immigrants were Jews. In 1820 there were roughly between 4,000 and 5,000 Jews in America. It is estimated that by 1850 there were between 40,000 and 50,000 and that by 1880 there were almost 10 times that many. What were the reasons for this large immigration?

The chief reason was economic necessity. The population of Europe had grown tremendously in the early nineteenth century, and the Jewish population, in spite of wars and massacres, and in some places bans on Jewish marriages, had grown even more in proportion to the general population. The Industrial Revolution, which had started in England and spread to the continent, favored only the rich entrepreneurs, both Christians and Jews. Thousands of peasants left their farms and villages and crowded into the cities to work in mills and factories. Others had gone to America. Very often the innkeepers, shopkeepers, and craftsmen in the villages had been Jews. When the countryside emptied, they were left without a source of livelihood. There was no place for them in the cities. The only solution was to emigrate. In doing this they had a precedent. Many adventurous young

38

men from Jewish families had left their homes to seek their fortunes in the New World. Ocean travel was becoming more common, and thousands of Jews from Germany, from western Poland, from Austria and Bohemia gathered in the Atlantic seaports — Bremen, Hamburg, Le Havre — and waited for ships to take them across the ocean.

Immigration societies were formed in Berlin, Vienna, and Prague to help the poorer immigrants. They traveled steerage, herded together among cattle and pigs, sleeping on wooden shelves arranged in tiers, eating food that was "hardly fit for cattle back in Bohemia," as one of the immigrants wrote in his diary. But the voyage lasted only a few weeks — after that came America, and the horizon was the limit.

The horizon lay to the west. Native Americans were crossing the mountains in covered wagons, staking out land in the western territories. The homesteads they left behind were taken over by German peasants, many of whom settled in Pennsylvania. German Jews settled among them, as they had in the old country. Others followed the wagon trails. They lacked the skills we usually attribute to pioneers. Since they hadn't been permitted to work on the land in Europe, they didn't know how to fell trees, plow the earth, or plant crops. Roadbuilding, mining, and what we call heavy industry had little attraction for them. It was difficult work with little recompense or chance for advancement. But the German-Jewish immigrants didn't lack an adventurous spirit. Distance didn't daunt them. They were willing to travel far, on foot if necessary, to endure hardships, to face loneliness. Most of the German Jews started out as peddlers, with a basket or pack on their back, filled with useful gadgets, cutlery, "notions" such as combs, scissors, needles, thread — anything and everything that the pioneer men and women might need. Yankee peddlers had preceded them. Farm women living far from towns were accustomed to dealing with itinerant vendors and welcomed their coming. Quite often they were European immigrants themselves and were glad to have a chance to talk to a peddler in their native language.

Some peddlers were more clever or perhaps luckier than others. They made enough money to buy a horse and buggy and a bigger stock of wares — perhaps farm implements, carpentry tools, pots and pans and dress materials for the women. If they came to a town or village that looked prosperous they opened a general store, a hardware store, or dry goods business. In a few years they saved up enough money to send for their wives and children, for brothers and sisters. They wrote letters to Frankfurt, to Strasbourg or Posen, urging friends to join them in the new land. Others, who were not so lucky, went on peddling on foot or sank to the level of hoboes and tramps. Their families back home perhaps never heard from them again.

The middle western cities were chosen by many German Jews. Cincinnati, Ohio, dates its first Jewish community from 1824, Louisville, Kentucky, from 1832, Chicago, Illinois, from 1837. Germans and German Jews came to Milwaukee and other cities in Wisconsin. Jewish immigrants followed the gold rush to California. In 1849, the year of the gold rush, a Yom Kippur service was held in a tent in San Francisco. In western mining towns Jewish merchants sold supplies to gold and silver prospectors. The heavy denim pants called levis were first manufactured by a Jewish peddler named Levi Strauss in California.

In 1848 revolutions broke out in nearly every country in Europe. The failure of the revolutions set off a new wave of immigration. Many of the German Jews who came to this country after 1848 were intellectuals — teachers, writers, musicians — who did much to enrich the cultural life of America. Their struggle against European monarchy made them value American democracy and wish to preserve it. They joined the abolitionist movement and fought in the Union armies during the Civil War.

Rabbi Isaac Mayer Wise (1819-1900), leader of Reform Judaism in the United States. Born in Bohemia and educated in Vienna, he came to America in 1846. Wise led a congregation in Cincinnati for 46 years, and worked to unify the Reform congregations in America.

Rabbi David Einhorn (1809-1879), born in Bavaria, came to Baltimore in 1855. He spoke out against slavery, and thus tangled with Rabbi Wise on that issue as well as on points of doctrine. Threatened by a proslavery mob, he left Baltimore in 1861. Einhorn later led Reform congregations in Philadelphia and New York.

But not all Jews were on the side of the North. Some who lived in the South favored the Confederacy. Judah P. Benjamin served under Jefferson Davis as Secretary of War and Secretary of State. Rabbi Isaac Mayer Wise of Cincinnati, a leader of the Reform Synagogue movement, sided with the South, and there were rabbis who quoted the Bible in their sermons to prove that slavery was divinely ordained. In opposition to them Rabbi David Einhorn of Baltimore preached in favor of abolition. On the subject of slavery and states' rights the Jews were as divided among themselves as the rest of the American people. Politically as well as economically the Jews had by the time of the Civil War been absorbed into the mainstream of American life. This was a far cry from the old European ghettos where the Jews had had no status as citizens at all, and could not voice their opinions on any matter that concerned the country they lived in.

For a reading on
Justice
see page 125.

For a reading on
Anti-Semitism
see page 141.

The nineteenth century was an era when most of the great American fortunes were made. It was still possible to go "from rags to riches" in one generation, to start like Andrew Carnegie as a bobbin boy, and end as a steel magnate. Some of the fortunes, mainly in retail business and to a smaller extent in manufacturing and banking, were made by Jewish immigrants from Germany who had started out as pack peddlers.

Nathan Straus (1848-1931) and his brother Isidor were partners in the R. H. Macy Company. During the panic of 1893, Nathan opened milk stations and lodging houses for the poor. He also led a 20-year campaign for the pasteurization of milk. His brother **Oscar Solomon Straus** (1850-1926) was a lawyer, diplomat, and cabinet member.

One of these men was Lazarus Straus, who came from Bavaria in 1852, and traveled through Georgia first with a peddler's pack, then with a horse and buggy. Then he opened a shop in Talbotton, Georgia, and sent for his wife and three small sons. After the Civil War, Lazarus Straus and his three sons, Isidor, Nathan, and Oscar, left Georgia and moved to New York where they opened a crockery business. In 1871 the Straus brothers rented a corner in the basement of Macy's department store for a china and glassware display. By 1888 they had become partners in the R. H. Macy Company and with imaginative merchandising skill turned it into a huge department store, which became the model for others. The Straus brothers were noted for their many civic and philanthropic activities. Oscar Straus was envoy to Turkey and Secretary of the Department of Commerce and Labor under President Theodore Roosevelt. A member of the third generation, Jesse Isidor Straus, became Ambassador to France. Adam Gimbel and Benjamin Altman also started as peddlers and became owners of large New York department stores.

Baiersdorf, Germany, was the birthplace of the seven Seligman brothers who began their business careers as peddlers in Alabama. Joseph Seligman was the first to come to America, in 1838, and his brothers followed him. Jesse lived in Selma, Alabama, and Joseph had a drygoods store in Greensboro. In 1862 they moved to New York and started a banking firm, which formed branches in New Orleans,

The banking firm of **Joseph Seligman** (1819-1880) provided financial aid to the Union during the Civil War. **Solomon R. Guggenheim** (1861-1949), one of Meyer Guggenheim's seven sons, founded a museum of nonobjective art in 1937. His fine collection of twentieth-century paintings was moved to Frank Lloyd Wright's structure on Fifth Avenue in 1959.

San Francisco, Frankfurt, London, and Paris. Joseph Seligman was a good friend of General Ulysses Grant and a staunch supporter of President Lincoln. His firm obtained loans in Europe for the United States Government and after the war continued to give financial support to the U.S. Navy. In a manner characteristic of the German Jews Joseph Seligman was the founder of such organizations as the Hebrew Orphan Home and an Ethical Culture Society. He was a member of the Board of Education in New York and president of the American Geographical Society.

Perhaps the most spectacular of the family fortunes was the one made by the Guggenheim brothers, of whom there were also seven. Their father, Meyer Guggenheim, came from a small town in Switzerland where his family had lived for 200 years. In 1847, Meyer, who was then 19, began to peddle merchandise with a horse and buggy in the coal mining towns of Pennsylvania. Later he manufactured lye and stove polish and sold imported Swiss embroideries. In the 1880's he invested in some silver and lead mines in Colorado, then in copper mines and smelters. It was in copper that the Guggenheim fortune was made.

His sons expanded the industry and became patrons of art, music, and the sciences. One of them endowed the Guggenheim fellowships. Another founded the Guggenheim Museum in New York to house his collection of modern paintings and sculpture.

6. *Religious and Community Life*

For a reading on
Community
see page 113.

In the European ghetto the synagogue was not only a place for worship, but a house of study as well. The body of accumulated knowledge was large. It contained not only religious doctrines and the history of the Jewish people, but rules governing everyday conduct, philosophical discussions, parables, folk tales, legends, and poetry. A child could begin by learning the Hebrew alphabet, go on to reading the Bible, and continue to study and discuss the more difficult books such as the Mishna and Talmud all through his life. Prayers were an everyday obligation, which could be performed either in the synagogue or at home. The rabbi did not necessarily lead in worship. Rather he was a leader of the community, a teacher and a judge. He would interpret the law and pass judgment on any question—from a divorce case or business dispute to a minute point of dietary law, such as whether a pot in which milk had been boiled could be used for cooking meat. He was also responsible for the community's welfare. Though the ghetto Jews paid taxes to the state, they got almost no benefits in return. They were responsible for their own charities. Indeed, their religion laid this obligation upon them. The Hebrew word *zedaka* for charity or benevolence, also means justice. To provide for the poor, the sick, and the aged was simply an act of justice.

For a reading on
Tsedakah
see page 123.

In America this pattern could not be duplicated, nor was it desirable. It had already begun to vanish in western Europe after the fall of the ghettos. The Jews adapted themselves to the laws and

Benjamin Altman (1840-1913). In 1906 he built his second department store at Fifth Avenue and 34th Street. B. Altman & Co. was so popular that it drew the rest of the New York shopping center uptown with it. Altman left his large collection of paintings to the Metropolitan Museum of Art.

Hebrew Union College in Cincinnati, Ohio. Founded in 1875
by Rabbi Isaac M. Wise, it is the oldest rabbinical school
in the United States.

customs of whatever country they lived in. In America this process
of adaptation came about naturally. When we speak of a "Jewish
community" in an American city we use the term in a loose sense.
It was only a community insofar as its members felt they shared certain traditions, customs, and religious observances, and wished to
preserve them.

We have seen how the early Jewish settlers bought burial plots so
their dead could be buried in consecrated ground. They continued to
do this in the nineteenth century. In the large cities there was more
than one Jewish cemetery. As immigration increased each group that
came tended to form its own little enclave. This was especially true of
the synagogues. By the time of the Civil War there were between 50
and 60 synagogues in New York alone, representing German, Polish,
Spanish, Dutch, Russian, English, and Bohemian Jews. Sometimes
the members of one European community or of one trade formed their
own congregation. If they couldn't afford a building, they rented a
vacant store or a basement in a tenement house.

The rapid growth of houses of worship extended to social life.
Since there was no central authority, no chief rabbi or council as
there had been in the past in Europe, the immigrants formed numerous mutual benefit societies or *chevras*. Some were quite small and
perhaps had only one function, such as visiting the sick, or providing
an insurance or loan fund for its members. Others enlarged their scope

and became social clubs as well, providing entertainment and often cultural activities such as literary discussion groups, choral societies, and orchestras. The young men's Hebrew literary societies of the nineteenth century gave rise much later to the Y.M.H.A.'s patterned somewhat on the Y.M.C.A.'s. There were also many fraternal orders established, similar to the Masons. Such an organization was the Independent Order of B'nai B'rith founded in 1843, with lodges in many cities. By 1860 it had a membership of 50,000.

In the 1850's and 1860's the German Jews began building hospitals in the larger cities. One reason for these hospitals was that Jewish patients who observed the dietary laws couldn't get kosher food in the general hospitals or those run by Christian denominations. Jewish orphanages and homes for the aged began to appear at that time. The history of Jewish charitable and welfare organizations is so complicated that we can only make a note of it here.

Education had been a matter of concern for the early settlers. The first synagogues tried to maintain schools for children, but Jewish parochial education never became widespread. In the 1840's when the compulsory public school system came into existence, Jewish children began to attend public schools, and the old synagogue schools dwindled and finally disappeared. In the 1860's the last barrier to public school education was overcome when schools no longer required attendance on Saturday, the Jewish Sabbath. For religious instruction Jewish children went to Sabbath or Sunday schools which were conducted in English, or to afternoon Hebrew schools which taught the Hebrew language, as well as religion. Both types of schools have always been voluntary.

For a reading on **'Education** *see page 130.*

The first synagogues in America followed the Sephardic ritual. This was an Orthodox ritual. In 1824 a group of 47 members of *Beth Elohim* congregation in Charleston, South Carolina, led by Isaac Harby, tried to institute some reforms in the ritual. They wanted to shorten the service, introduce English into the prayerbook, and have the rabbi give a sermon in English. When the trustees refused this request, they seceded and formed their own congregation. Eight years later they returned, but by that time "reform" was in the air.

46

The Jews arriving from Germany had been influenced by the Reform movement which had started in Hamburg and Berlin. One of the innovations of that movement was the introduction of organ music. This was a hotly debated question, since the Orthodox synagogues had allowed only choral music. In the Orthodox synagogue women sat in a separate section from the men, usually in the balcony. The men wore some sort of head covering, and a prayer shawl. No part of the service was in the vernacular language, and there was no "sermon" in the modern sense of the word. The proponents of Reform argued that to many worshipers the Hebrew prayers were meaningless and that the whole ritual was antiquated.

For a reading on **Religion** see page 118.

In their zeal to modernize the ritual they threw a great deal of it overboard. The Reform temples were in many ways closer to some Protestant churches than to the old synagogues. So much so, that the East European Jews often recoiled from them in horror. This was not the "old-time religion" as they knew it. The classic façades of the temples fronted by pillars, the stained glass windows, choir lofts, organs, the sermon in English seemed alien to them. They continued to worship in their accustomed fashion, or to make compromises between the old and the new. Out of the conflicts of the nineteenth century there emerged the three large divisions of organized Jewish religion—Reform, Conservative, and Orthodox. Each of them has changed with the changing times. The Reform temples have re-introduced some of the old customs and the others have modernized some of theirs.

For a reading on **Religion** see page 119.

For a reading on **Religion** see page 119.

The Jews from Eastern Europe: 1880-1924

1. *Russia and the Jewish Pale of Settlement*

In the latter part of the nineteenth century, when immigrants began pouring into this country at an unprecedented rate, the largest single group, next to the Italians, were the Jews from Eastern Europe. They came from a scattered area—thousands, for instance, came from Rumania and the Austrian province of Galicia, but by far the largest number came from Russia, or to be more exact, from the Jewish Pale of Settlement in the Russian empire.

What was this Pale of Settlement? Historically it was not very old—it had only existed since the latter part of the eighteenth century. In earlier times few Jews had lived in Russia proper. Only rarely were Jewish merchants from Poland and Germany allowed temporary entry to the great Russian trading fairs. Even Peter the Great (1682-1725), who imported German, Dutch, and English shipbuilders, stonemasons, mechanics, and merchants to help him westernize his backward country, excluded the Jews. During the eighteenth century era of enlightenment in the West, Russia was still a feudal country with an autocratic Czar, a powerful Greek Orthodox Church, a small landed nobility, and millions of serfs attached to the land. At the close of that century, when the American people had declared their independence from Great Britain, and the French people overthrew the Bourbon monarchy, Catherine the Great of Russia expanded her empire by annexing most of Poland. In the Ukraine, the Baltic countries, and Poland lived one million Jews. At practically one stroke they became Russian subjects. What was to be done with them? The Czarina, Catherine, solved the problem by defining a boundary beyond which they might not go. This border area into which the Jews were confined became known as the Jewish Pale of Settlement.

Catherine the Great (1729-1796) became Czarina of Russia in 1762. Under Catherine, Russia expanded westward, taking over the rest of the Ukraine and most of Poland. On December 21, 1791, Catherine established the Jewish Pale of Settlement.

The Czars who followed Catherine the Great—Alexander I, Nicholas I, and Alexander II—kept shifting their policies in respect to the Jews. At times the Pale was enlarged, then it was restricted again. A decree would go out that the Jews leave the rural areas and move into the towns. Then the decree was revoked. Jews were allowed to have homes in some towns, others required special permits. A permit might be good for only 24 hours, and if a man was caught out of bounds, he had to pay a fine. Russian officials were open to bribes, and the Jews learned to live with a corrupt government.

At one time the Jews had their own self-governing bodies or *kahals*. These kahals were now stripped of all their powers except that of collecting taxes. And the taxes imposed on the Jews were twice as high as those for other groups. The government policy toward education kept shifting also. Nicholas I had a minister who argued that the only way to absorb the Jews was to educate them. For this purpose "crown" schools were established. At first the Jews welcomed them, but it soon became apparent that the main function of these schools was not to educate but to make converts. A decree went out that the Jews select rabbis to conduct government business—issue birth certificates, perform marriages, officiate at funerals, settle legal disputes. These were called "crown rabbis," and since they were puppets of the government, they were extremely unpopular with the people. Whenever they could, the Jews tried to avoid the decrees,

The Jewish Pale of Settlement in the late nineteenth century included 15 provinces of western Russia, as well as Russian Poland. The rest of Russia was closed to Jews, except for doctors and certain merchants who were allowed to live in some cities of the interior. The Pale was officially abolished during the Russian Revolution of March 1917.

some of which, if properly carried out, might have been to their ultimate advantage. Instead of availing themselves of "crown" benefits, they stubbornly maintained their own schools, went to their own rabbis for advice and the settling of disputes, and organized their own welfare societies.

The law that was hardest to evade was the compulsory military service. In Russia during the first half of the nineteenth century men had to serve in the army for 25 years. A cruel law by any standards, it had an additional feature in the case of the Jews, which made it barbaric. Jewish boys were conscripted at the age of 12 instead of 18, and had to spend six years in a "cantonment" in order to be indoctrinated into the Greek Orthodox faith before they began their 25 years of military service. Parents whose sons were taken into service mourned them as dead. Even if a man survived the brutal life of the army camps and didn't die on the battlefield, he came out after 31 years a complete stranger to his own people. Nobody sent his child willingly. Since every town or village had to produce a certain number of recruits, gangs of *chappers* (kidnapers) roamed the countryside and literally snatched children away. If a rumor came that a gang of kidnapers had been seen, parents hid their boys in the woods or even had them crippled or maimed. This law was so difficult to carry out that eventually the Russian government had to modify it. In 1855 during the reign of Alexander II, the 25-year term of service was changed to six years and the "cantonment" was done away with. It seemed to the Jews that a new and better day was dawning. When in 1861 Czar Alexander II freed the serfs all of Russia rejoiced, including the Jews, of whom there were almost three million now. They felt that the new Czar was truly a liberator.

This was not entirely the case. When 47 million serfs were set free, their masters were compensated for their loss, but the serfs themselves were not given any land. They only swelled the great mass of landless, impoverished Russian *muzhiks* (peasants) who lived in squalid huts together with the pigs and cattle. They could neither read nor write, and believed anything the village priest chose to tell them.

Alexander II and his advisers, like the German rulers a century before, were astute enough to see that the Jews could be useful. The domicile laws were relaxed in some cases to allow the wealthier Jews and those who qualified as skilled mechanics to establish residence in Moscow and a few other cities in Russia proper. The "crown" schools were abandoned and a certain number of Jewish students were allowed to enter the regular gymnazia (high schools) and universities. A Jewish professional class came into existence — doctors, lawyers, teachers, engineers. Some went abroad to study and came back from

Alexander II (1818-1881) became Czar of Russia in 1855. He freed the serfs in 1861 and undertook partial reforms of the courts, the army, and local government. Problems of land distribution caused discontent and led to Alexander's assassination by a terrorist in 1881.

Rural villagers of the Ukraine.

England or Germany with liberal ideas. In 1863 a Polish rebellion, in which Jews also took part, was crushed. Political "criminals" were exiled to Siberia. Others left the country. But the mass of the Jewish people was not affected. Political rebellion at that time was a luxury for the educated and comparatively well-to-do. Most of the Jews simply wanted to be left alone. These were the millions who lived packed together as tightly as "herring in a barrel" throughout the towns and villages of the Pale of Settlement.

2. Village Life

The typical Jewish village or small town of the Russian Pale differed from the sixteenth century ghetto of western Europe. It was not enclosed like a fortress by a stone wall. Rather it was set off from the rest of the world by an invisible barrier made up of folk customs, religious observance, and a close-knit community and family life. Most of the people were poor. They worked as cobblers, tailors, carpenters, glaziers, draymen. A few kept taverns or small shops. A man who had neither a trade nor a shop might travel about the countryside with a horse and wagon or even on foot to see what he could find for a small bit of money. He might pick up a rusty plow which he could clean, or a piece of lumber, and exchange it with a peasant for a bag of grain, or other produce to take to the market. He seldom traveled so far that he couldn't get back to his family before the Sabbath.

For a reading on *Integration* see page 135.

The Sabbath began on Friday after sundown. No matter how poor a family was, even if it lived on potatoes and cabbage all week, some coins were set aside to buy fish or meat and a white loaf for the Friday evening and Sabbath dinner. The men hurried to the synagogue for evening prayer. The children had been bathed and dressed in their best clothes. The women, who had scrubbed and cooked during the day, now lit the Friday night candles. Up and down the narrow streets from every window these candles glimmered. The good smell of food cooking filled the house. There was a saying that a person could starve any day of the week, but nobody had ever starved on the Sabbath. Even the town's paupers and tramps, who slept on synagogue benches and lived on handouts, were assured of one hot meal during the week. For it was a duty, even an honor, to share the Sabbath meal with a guest. If a stranger arrived in town or was stranded during a journey (traveling was forbidden on the Sabbath) he went to the synagogue knowing that someone would offer him hospitality.

For a reading on
Religion
see page 120.

Families were large, with three generations often living under one roof. Marriages were arranged by the parents of young people, often with the help of a professional matchmaker. Perhaps the father

For a reading on
Family
see page 115.

A carriage-maker (left) and a cobbler, both of Warsaw.

A *cheder*, or elementary Hebrew school. The
melamed's elderly father is seated at the left.

returned from a journey with good news; "*Mazel tov* (congratulations),
Rachel," he said to his daughter, "you're engaged to be married."
Rachel didn't dare ask to whom. Very often the betrothed couple
didn't see each other before the wedding. "Time enough to get acquainted later," the old people said in jest, which was tinged with
sadness. They knew that life would be hard. There was hardly such a
thing as a carefree time of youth. In Jewish law divorce was allowed,
but it was not very common. The birth of a child was a happy occasion
and small children were tenderly cared for. But school began early, at
the age of five, sometimes sooner. Boys were sent to *cheder* (elementary Hebrew school) where they studied from early morning until
dark with little free time for play. The *melamed* (teacher) was often
underpaid and burdened with cares of his own, and he was expected
to exercise authority. He dealt out slaps and cuffs indiscriminately.

Though the countryside was not far away, Jewish children seldom
went swimming or fishing or roaming in the woods. Some of the holidays, however, brought nature to them. During the fall holiday
Sukkoth, every family built its own little *sukkah* or hut and decorated
it with branches and autumn fruits. *Lag b'omer*, a holiday in early
summer, was similar to Arbor Day. The winter holidays had their
own kind of merrymaking and were a welcome release from school.

For a reading on
Education
see page 130.

We see from this that piety and learning were held in highest regard; they were more important than wealth. It was not at all rare for a man to devote his whole life to study and prayer. A young man who devoted himself to studying the Torah and Talmud might have a father or father-in-law who supported him and his family. Often his wife earned the family living. There were many capable and energetic women, who not only managed their households and raised their children, but operated a business of some kind, perhaps a tavern or shop. Women were not given a voice in community affairs and they sat apart from the men in the synagogue, but they were respected and honored in the family circle. This was during a time when a Russian peasant's wife was considered her husband's property and wife-beating was not only common but sanctioned by law. The Jews differed in other ways from their peasant neighbors. Drunkenness, the peasant's way of finding release from a life of toil, was rare among the Jews. So were crimes of violence, such as murder. Life in every form was held sacred.

These traits which characterized the Jews of the Pale of Settlement — a willingness to work hard and subsist on little, loyalty to family ties, regard for learning, rigid piety, and a moral obligation toward life — they brought with them to the New World.

For a reading on
Education
see page 131.

For a reading on
Education
see page 131.

For a reading on
Religion
see page 120.

A grandfather teaches his small grandson to read.

Gesia Street in the Jewish quarter of Warsaw. After the pogroms of the 1880's many Russian Jews settled in Warsaw. By the eve of World War II Warsaw had a Jewish community of 370,000 — the largest in Europe.

3. *The Immigrants*

Alexander II was assassinated in 1881, and his successor, Alexander III, took stern measures to crush any hint of rebellion. The various nationality groups within the Russian Empire — Polish, Latvian, German — were forbidden the use of their native languages in the schools. Strict censorship was imposed on books and newspapers. Loyalty to "Mother Russia" became the watchword, and Mother Russia was synonymous with the Czar's government. The Jews bore the brunt of the attack. The Russian peasants were incited by village priests and officials, and bloody massacres, or *pogroms*, broke out all over the Pale of Settlement. After the turn of the century armed gangs called "The Black Hundreds" marched against the Jewish villages with religious banners, portraits of the Czar, and the cry of "Down with the Jews!"

In May 1882 the Czar issued a set of Temporary Rules, which became known as the "May Laws" and which threw the life of the Pale into chaos. These laws were complicated, but in general they were intended to break up the Jewish villages and small towns and force the inhabitants to move into larger towns, which were already intolerably congested. For example, Jews were not allowed to settle "anew" in another village, even if they had inherited property in it or wanted to join their families. Local authorities were given the right to expel any Jews they didn't want and to seize their homes. In some places the Jews had been allowed to work at a craft but not to engage in business. This rule was now interpreted to mean that a man could produce something, but not sell it. Thousands lost their means of livelihood. The schools and universities lowered their quotas so that it was almost impossible for a Jew to enter a Russian school. Jewish lawyers were not admitted to the bar, and doctors were hedged in by restrictions.

Alexander III (1845-1894) became Czar of Russia after his father's assassination in 1881. His repressive measures set off a mass emigration of Jews from Russia.

In 1891 when the Grand Duke Sergei became Governor of Moscow he gave an order that all the Jews leave the city at once. Between 15,000 and 20,000 Jews of Moscow were rounded up and escorted out of town under police guard. Where would all these displaced and unemployed people go? As the Czar's minister, Pobedonetsev, cynically remarked, one third would die, one third would leave the country, and the rest would become absorbed into the general population, that is, lose their identity as Jews.

At least one part of his prediction came true. Hundreds of thousands of destitute and desperate people began leaving the country. They were granted exit permits, but since these required long waits and bureaucratic red tape, many crossed the borders secretly at night. They streamed into the border towns of Germany and Austria. The Jews of these countries became dismayed at the masses of refugees, hungry, ragged, and often ill from exposure, who looked to them for assistance. The German Jews at first tried to stem the tide, to plead with these people to go back. They sent delegations to the Czar to intercede on their behalf. When fresh pogroms broke out, such as the

For a reading on *Anti-Semitism* *see page 142.*

57

A rare photograph of a group of young revolutionaries gathered before the body of a friend killed in the Kishinev pogrom of 1903.

For a reading on
Anti-Semitism
see page 143.

Kishinev pogrom of 1903, heads of foreign governments, including President Theodore Roosevelt, sent notes of protest to the Czar. The protests were ignored. The Jews of western Europe began helping the refugees. The *Alliance Israelite Universelle*, which had been formed a few decades before to help victims of cholera epidemics, now sent committees to the border towns to help the refugees with money, clothing, and medical care.

The Russian Jews scattered over western Europe and England. Since ocean travel had improved and steerage accommodations were less primitive than they had been, many emigrated overseas to South America, South Africa, and Canada. But for most of them the ultimate goal was the United States of America. About two-thirds of the ocean liners which carried immigrants docked in New York harbor.

For a reading on
Integration
see page 136.

Before entering New York the immigrants had to undergo an examination at Ellis Island. Congress was trying to keep out undesirables and there was always the danger of being sent back. To people weary from the long journey and afraid of anything "official" this was a terrifying ordeal. There were organizations to help them, notably

58

Three students who were active in self-defense measures during the Kishinev pogrom, 1905. Morris Lerner (left) later emigrated to South Dakota where he established a farm under the Homestead Act. Ben and Nathan Gelfand became grocers in Minneapolis.

HIAS (Hebrew Immigrant Aid Society) which sometimes provided interpreters. The language they had to interpret was usually Yiddish.

If he passed the physical examination and answered successfully a long list of questions, the immigrant's passport was stamped and he was ready to leave Ellis Island for the Barge Office at the tip of Manhattan Island.

For a reading on
Tsedakah
see page 123.

Inspectors examine the eyes of immigrants. Ellis Island, 1913.

4. *New York's East Side—People at Work*

The saying was, "In America people rake up gold in the streets." The immigrants didn't believe this as a literal fact, but even as a symbol it was no longer true. The limitless horizon was gone. The frontier had been settled; the great fortunes had been made. By the 1880's America was becoming increasingly urban, and the new Jewish immigrants, instead of setting out for the road with a peddler's pack, congregated in the large cities—New York, Philadelphia, Boston, Chicago. A few had the dream of "going back to the land," and joined cooperative farming communities, in South Dakota, Oregon, the Middle West. With the exception of some in New Jersey these didn't last long.

For a reading on **Integration** *see page 137.*

Sabbath eve in a cellar. Photograph by Jacob A. Riis, 1890.

A newcomer wandering around New York, frightened and dazzled by the tall buildings and bustling crowds, deafened by the roar of the elevated train, might run by chance into a landsman (townsman) from the old country, who told him about opportunities in St. Paul, Minnesota, or Atlanta, Georgia, where life moved at a slower tempo. He listened and risked his few dollars on a train ticket. More often than not he remained in New York.

Pushcart peddler. In 1898 an estimated 1,500 peddlers sold their wares on the Lower East Side. Each cart had a specialty — clothing or crockery, fruit or pickles, boots or fish.

The reasons for staying in New York were simple. A man with little money and a family to support had to find work and a place to stay right away. In proportion to their number there were more women and children among the Jewish immigrants than among other groups. Before laws were passed to prohibit contract labor, groups of men had come from the Slavic countries to work on railroads and in mines. The Jews didn't do this. They brought their families and came to stay. On the East Side of New York they found work as cigar-makers, garment workers, and pushcart peddlers. A dignified old man with a beard and a skullcap who had sat over the Torah in his native town might be seen selling pretzels on Hester or Rivington Street. Another man sat bent over a sewing machine 17 hours a day, or stood at a pressing board pushing a heavy steam iron back and forth. Young girls worked in crowded factories which were draughty in winter and stifling in summer, and a health and fire hazard at all times. Men earned between six and ten dollars a week, women and girls between four and five dollars. This type of work was called "the sweatshop system."

It was not really a system at all, since it had grown up in a haphazard fashion. Earlier in the century clothing had been custom-tailored or sewed at home. The invention of heavy sewing machines and steam presses, and the increased demand for ready-to-wear clothing had given rise to the garment industry. Since the manufacture of clothing required less outlay of capital than heavy industry, it had attracted

For a reading on
Justice
see page 125.

"I cash clothes." Many immigrants were too old to learn a new trade or too poor to set up a shop. They supported themselves by buying and selling old clothes.

For a reading on
Justice
see page 126.

For a reading on
Justice
see page 127.

the earlier Jewish immigrants from Germany, who by the latter part of the century owned most of the garment factories. The owners, instead of carrying out the whole manufacturing process, divided it up with contractors. The factory-owners employed skilled cutters who cut out the garments on their premises, then sent the bundles of cuttings to the contractors, who in turn hired workers to do the basting, sewing, pressing, and finishing. The contractors rented a loft in a rickety building, or used their own tenement flats as shops, crowding machines and workers into every available corner. If the workers complained they were told to leave. There were plenty of fresh immigrants coming off the ships every day to take their place. The contractors were not necessarily cruel and inhuman. They were themselves the victims of a wasteful and chaotic method of production.

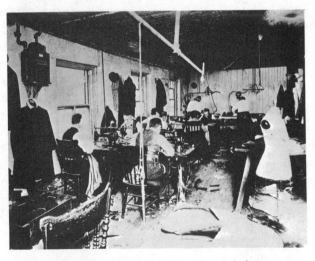

Sweatshop, 1910. A garment was usually made by a team of three: the machine operator, the baster, and the finisher.

Moe Levy & Co. Clothing Factory, about 1912. The factory system was faster than the shop system. Each worker made only one part of the garment, over and over again.

Every now and then something happened that brought to the notice of the public the appalling conditions of the sweatshops. On March 25, 1911, a fire broke out at the Triangle Waist Company, which employed girl workers. Several girls jumped to their death from a seventh floor loft and 146 died in the fire. Later the states began enacting safety legislation, but meanwhile the workers themselves had begun to organize unions which eventually reduced the work week to 40 hours, raised the wages, and improved working conditions.

The labor movement had been growing all over the country. In 1881 several craft unions joined together under the leadership of Samuel Gompers, a Jewish cigar-maker from London, into an association which gave rise to the American Federation of Labor. The "needle trades," as the garment trades were sometimes called, went through a long trial-and-error period until they formed the two giant trade unions. The workers in men's clothing formed the Amalgamated Clothing Workers of America, in 1914, with Sidney Hillman as president. He held this post until his death in 1946. In the 1930's Hillman became one of the founders of the CIO (Congress of Industrial Organizations) and he was one of President Roosevelt's advisers during the New Deal.

The other great union, the International Ladies' Garment Workers (ILGWU), was founded in 1900 and took part in 1910 in a strike which lasted two months, involved 60,000 workers, and resulted in a history-making settlement, called "The Protocol of Peace." The man who negotiated this settlement was Louis D. Brandeis, then a Boston lawyer, who was later to become a Justice of the Supreme Court. This settlement provided for an Arbitration Board, Grievance Committees and other innovations which later became standard practice in labor-management relations.

For a reading on
Justice
see page 127.

The two great garment workers unions, the Amalgamated, under Sidney Hillman, and the ILGWU under David Dubinsky, pioneered in other matters concerning labor. They had a system of unemployment insurance before the Federal government took over that function. They also started a program of auxiliary service for the workers. They built cooperative, low cost apartments, established health centers, nurseries, and summer camps, as well as adult education classes, and lecture and concert series. *Pins and Needles*, with book by Marc Blitzstein and songs by Harold Rome and others, was put on with a cast made up entirely of garment workers of the ILGWU in 1937. It had songs of social protest in the style of the thirties, such as "Sing Me a Song of Social Significance," and after Chamberlain's Munich pact, "Britannia Waives the Rules," as well as catchy boy-meets-girl love songs. Planned originally as a week-end entertainment for union members, it made stage history by becoming the most successful musical to that date and played on Broadway for three years.

The greatest accomplishment of the unions, of course, was that they abolished the sweatshop system. In recent years, the membership, which had been made up of East European Jewish immigrants, was in large part replaced by Italians, Negroes, and Puerto Ricans. But the leaders of the garment unions have often been Jews who had started as workers in the shops.

Sidney Hillman (1887-1946), president of the Amalgamated Clothing Workers from 1914 until his death. He came from Lithuania in 1907. **David Dubinsky** (right) became president of the ILGWU in 1932. A Pole, he came to America in 1911 after escaping from a Siberian prison.

Sunday in the Park—a scene from *Pins and Needles*, staged by garment workers in 1937.

5. *The People's Speech*

Hebrew, the language of ancient Palestine and of modern Israel, was for the immigrants the language of the Bible, the Talmud, and the book of prayer. Their everyday speech was Yiddish. Hebrew and Yiddish have the same alphabet, and on the printed and written page they look almost alike. But the spoken languages are quite different from each other.

As the Jews moved about from place to place, they learned the language of each country. The Sephardim, besides speaking Spanish, used among themselves a language that was a mixture of Spanish and Hebrew and was written in Hebrew characters. This was called Ladino. In the Middle Ages in Germany the Jews began speaking the local dialect—Middle High German. Again, they mixed Hebrew words with it, and wrote it in Hebrew. This was the language they brought with them to Eastern Europe. Since the German word for Jew, *Jude*, became *Yid* in Eastern Europe, the language was called *Yiddish*. In Poland and Russia the language acquired many Slavic words, but it remained basically Germanic.

For many centuries in Europe the Yiddish language was not held in high esteem. It was called "jargon," literally gibberish. Scholars and serious writers wrote their books in Hebrew, just as medieval scholars had written in Latin, scorning the vernacular languages of their day. But a vernacular, or everyday language, becomes stronger

Sholom Aleichem was the pen name of Solomon Rabinowitz (1859-1916), Yiddish author best known for his short stories about life in the villages of the Russian Pale. With his family he left Kiev after the pogrom of 1905, and came to America in 1914. His name means "Peace Unto You."

and richer with use. That is what happened to Yiddish. At first it was considered only suitable for doggerel verses, light romances, and folk tales. It became a literary language when in the latter part of the nineteenth century writers began using it for lyric poetry, plays, stories, and novels. Its former drawbacks became its virtues. Since it was a mixture to begin with, it was flexible and easily incorporated new words and phrases. Because it had been used by ordinary people — laborers, draymen, peddlers, and vagabonds — it had a strong, earthy quality. What it lacked in grammatical complexity, it made up in a varied vocabulary. Though it had been lightly dismissed as "women's language" and "kitchen talk," it was not trivial. Women did more than exchange gossip. They sang lullabies to their children. Grandmothers talked about the old days in the little towns, about flights and pogroms, about sons who had been impressed into the army or had run off to America. And so the language had a strain of tenderness and melancholy. It also had wit, and a wry kind of humor. The Jews, who had survived so many upheavals and disasters, had learned to turn a phrase into a joke upon themselves.

As the immigrants began learning English, they mingled English words and phrases with their Yiddish. The children and grandchildren, born in America, spoke English almost exclusively. But as the use of the Yiddish language declined, a strange thing began to happen. Yiddish words and phrases cropped up on the stage, in novels, and more recently on radio and in television. Some became current usage and have been included in American language dictionaries. A recent magazine article has this title: "Around the World with Thumb and Chutzpah." We all know what "thumb" means to a traveler. *Chutzpah,*

For a reading on
Family
see page 116.

a Yiddish word of Hebrew origin, meaning insolence or impudence, has been mellowed by usage to mean a jolly kind of daring or nerve.

6. *The Yiddish Press*

In an era when newspapers were numerous and highly competitive the Yiddish language press was no exception. It has been estimated that at one time there were 12 Yiddish papers published in New York alone, and that their combined circulation was over half a million. It was the largest and most diversified of any foreign language press. Yiddish weeklies and monthlies had been started in the 1870's, but the first daily paper, the *Tageblatt* (Jewish Daily News), came out in 1885 and lasted 43 years before it merged with other papers. It was believed to be the first Yiddish daily in the world. The Yiddish papers reflected every shade of political opinion, from the conservative and religion-oriented *Tageblatt* and *Morning Journal* to the Zionist *Day*, the socialist *Forward* (est. 1897), the communist *Freiheit* (1922) and smaller philosophical-anarchist papers. These papers carried on a constant rivalry among themselves, not only in print but in arguments among the editors, writers, and intellectuals who gathered in the East Side cafés to drink tea and discuss the issues of the day.

The Jewish Daily Forward, September 15, 1897. In the cartoon Czar Nicholas II, surrounded by bodies, tries to strike a bargain with Uncle Sam.

For a reading on
Education
see page 132.

Though printed in Yiddish, the only language their public knew, the papers were far from parochial or narrow. Their aim was to educate the new immigrants and to help them become Americanized. Besides national and international news, they printed articles on American government and history, instructions on how to become naturalized citizens, news about unions, clubs, and fraternal organizations, and articles on popular science. Every paper printed letters from readers asking for advice on domestic problems. Of these the *Forward's Bintel Brief* (Bundle of Letters) became the best known. The Yiddish dailies and weeklies devoted more space to literature than American papers. They printed translations of European and American classics, and novels by Yiddish writers in daily installments. Among the working people in the ghetto there were many self-taught poets and writers who contributed poems, short stories, and essays dealing with the everyday lives of the immigrants. There were also well-educated journalists who produced book reviews and drama criticism of a high caliber.

For a reading on
Family
see page 116.

Among the Yiddish journalists Abraham Cahan (1860-1951) stands out. He had graduated from a teachers' institute in Vilno, Lithuania, and taught elementary school for a short time, until his participation in revolutionary activity made it difficult for him to remain in Russia. He came to New York in 1882, and worked at various odd jobs—as a cigarmaker, a teacher, editor of a small weekly paper—until in 1897 he helped found *The Jewish Daily Forward.* He left this paper to work for an American newspaper, *The Commercial Advertiser,* but returned in 1902 as editor and built up the *Forward* into a great newspaper with a circulation of 200,000 at its peak. Cahan was deeply concerned about the problems of the sweatshop workers and he did a great deal, both as an editor and a speaker, to help the unions which were at that time trying to get a foothold. Politically, the *Forward* was a socialist paper with moderate leanings.

The *Commercial Advertiser,* on which Cahan worked for several years, was a lively, crusading New York paper edited by Lincoln Steffens, who later became known as a "muckraking" reformer and wrote books exposing corruption and graft in big city politics. At the *Advertiser* Abraham Cahan met and became friendly with a young writer, Hutchins Hapgood, who had been born in Illinois, but was of old New England stock and had graduated from Harvard. When Hapgood was given an assignment to write a series of sketches about the Jewish immigrants of the East Side, it was Cahan who acted as his guide and interpreter. Cahan introduced him to old Hebrew scholars, fiery young Russian radicals, workingmen and shop girls, artists and actors and writers. Hutchins Hapgood's sketches were published in book form in 1902 and reprinted in 1967, under the title *Spirit of the Ghetto*. Hapgood was lucky in finding just the right illustrator, a young Jewish artist named Jacob Epstein, who sketched portraits of East Side characters. He lived and worked in the garret of a tenement overlooking Hester Street, in the heart of the ghetto. Jacob Epstein later moved to England, where he became a renowned sculptor, and was knighted.

Cahan wrote and published stories and novels in English. In 1917 he published *The Rise of David Levinsky*, which has become a classic of Jewish immigrant life. It is possible that the title was suggested to him by the title of an earlier American classic, *The Rise of Silas Lapham*, by William Dean Howells, which came out in 1885. *Silas Lapham* dealt with the conflict between an enterprising Yankee

Going to the Synagogue. A charcoal drawing by Jacob Epstein from Hutchins Hapgood's *The Spirit of the Ghetto*, 1902.

69

businessman and old Boston aristocracy. Howells, the editor of the *Atlantic Monthly* and *Harper's* for many years, knew Cahan and encouraged him in his writing. By helping each other, and collaborating when the opportunity arose, these writers and artists were weaving a new strand into the texture of American life.

7. *The Yiddish Theatre*

The East Side Jew's favorite form of entertainment was the theatre. The pool halls, saloons, and hangouts of the Bowery—the poor man's usual places of amusement—had little attraction for him. This doesn't mean that the theatre was necessarily of a serious or uplifting nature. On the contrary. The early Yiddish theatre consisted of melodramas interspersed with vaudeville acts, light operas based on Biblical and historical subjects, sentimental sketches, and broad farce. Later, under the influence of serious playwrights and of such actors as Jacob Adler and Maurice Schwartz, a realistic element was added in "slice-of-life" plays which presented the true life of the ghetto. But whatever the play was—tragedy or comedy or farce—the audience participated with gusto. They laughed, cried, hissed, cheered, and applauded the actors. On weekend nights whole families turned out, including children and babies in arms. During intermissions they bought souvenirs and refreshments, talked with old friends and met new ones. In its popular appeal the Yiddish theatre was not unlike the Elizabethan theatre of Shakespeare's day.

The history of the Yiddish theatre has been traced to the synagogue ritual. The Talmud forbade theatre as a form of "idol worship," but the Jews had always loved music, especially vocal music. In the synagogue the service was conducted by a cantor, who sang or chanted the prayer, with emphatic intonations, while the congregation made a rhythmic response. Some European cantors had developed a highly individual style, and people came a great distance to hear them. Such a cantor was young Zelig (later Sigmund) Mogalesco, the cantor at the Bucharest synagogue. He had been a child prodigy, had traveled through Rumania and southern Russia, and had led a choir of 20 men at the age of 14.

Grand Street Theatre, about 1900.

In 1876 a man named Abraham Goldfaden heard him sing and decided that the young cantor had not only a remarkable voice but a talent for acting. Goldfaden was a Russian Jew with a talent for writing and singing. After he had failed in business, he became a sort of music-hall performer; he wrote poems, set the words to popular tunes, and sang in Rumanian taverns. Goldfaden wrote a play and persuaded young Mogalesco, who was then 20, and several members of the synagogue choir to make up the cast. The play was an immediate success, and the troupe began touring various towns in Rumania and Russia. Since women were not allowed on the stage, Mogalesco often played women's parts with great success. He developed a talent for comedy. In a few years Goldfaden had enlarged his repertory and was hiring women as well as men.

In 1883 the Russian government outlawed the Yiddish theatre on the pretext that it was a hotbed of political intrigue. Immigration to America had already started and Goldfaden's troupe went to New York, where a ready-made audience awaited them. He hired a theatre which he called the Rumania. Other acting groups arrived from Europe and soon there was the Germania, the People's, the Windsor, the Thalia, and others, playing to full houses on the Bowery. Forgetting the old Talmudic injunction against "idol worship," the theatre lovers almost worshipped their favorite actors. One of the matinee idols of the day was Boris Thomashefsky, a dark, handsome, rather heavy-set man with curly black hair and a simpering manner who played romantic leads. The European-bred audiences preferred their stars, both male and female, to be on the plump side, in the style of early opera singers.

Jacob P. Adler (1855-1926), father of a theatrical family, toured Russia with Goldfaden's troupe and came to America in 1887. One of his greatest roles was in the Jewish *King Lear*. (Right) sheet music from *Lear*.

To satisfy the growing demand several playwrights turned out plays by the hundred, often borrowing from novels and other plays. Shakespeare was popular on the Yiddish stage, both in straight translation and in adaptations. There was a Yiddish version of *Hamlet* and *Othello* and a Jewish *King Lear*. Ibsen's *The Doll's House* had its counterpart in a play called *Minna* in which the heroine did more than slam the door on her loutish husband. She committed suicide by drinking carbolic acid. *God, Man and the Devil* was adapted from Goethe's *Faust*. After the turn of the century Jewish playwrights were producing original plays based on Jewish life and folklore. In the 1920's there were 12 Yiddish theatres in New York and several in other large cities, as well as numerous touring companies. They produced a number of excellent actors, some of whom later distinguished themselves in the American theatre.

Paul Muni (1895-1967), born in Austria, made his stage debut in Cleveland at the age of 12 in a Yiddish skit called *Two Corpses at Breakfast*. He joined Maurice Schwartz's Jewish Art Theatre in 1918, and in 1928 he went to Hollywood. A great character actor, Muni won an Oscar for *The Life of Louis Pasteur*.

Herschel Bernardi traveled the Yiddish theatre circuit with his parents and spoke his first onstage lines at the age of three. Among his television roles was that of Lt. Jacobi in *Peter Gunn*. Bernardi played Tevye for two years in the Broadway production of *Fiddler on the Roof*.

8. *Food*

What are knishes? Kreplach? Kneidlach? You will find them all under the letter K in the index of a Jewish cookbook, or you can order them in a Jewish restaurant. In some places knishes are sold like hot dogs or pizza and eaten out of hand. They are a kind of baked pastry filled with chopped meat, mashed potato, or a mixture of both. Kreplach are triangle-shaped pockets of noodle dough usually filled with chopped meat (though there are cheese kreplach too) and served like noodles or dumplings in soup. Kneidlach are dumplings of various types; the best known are the matzo balls served in chicken soup.

The above trio, like most Jewish foods, are derived from Central or East European sources. Sometimes you can guess the origin of a dish by its name. Blintzes are thin pancakes filled with cottage cheese, and folded like little plump pillows, then fried in butter and served with sour cream. They are related to Russian blini. Borscht, a soup made of beets and served cold, with sour cream, is a variant of one of the many kinds of Russian *Borshch* or Polish *Barshch*. Hot cabbage borscht, made with meat stock and containing a number of other vegetables, is none other than the hearty cabbage soup of the Russian peasant. Buckwheat kasha (*kasha* means cereal) and buckwheat pancakes come from Eastern Europe where buckwheat was cultivated. Rumanian *mamaliga,* on the other hand, resembles American cornmeal mush. Indian maize, or corn, was imported to Rumania from America and became a staple of that country's diet. Another dish from Rumania is an appetizer made of eggplant, which has been first broiled over a flame to give it a characteristic smoky flavor.

Yonah Shimmel's Knishery on Houston Street in New York City. Established in 1910, the knishery is now run by the founder's grandson.

Strudel, a rich pastry which is served at every Jewish wedding and celebration, is of Austrian origin. Making the paper-thin "stretch dough" for strudel is a culinary art developed by Viennese pastry cooks. Cheese cake, honey cake, and kichel (cookies) come from Central or Eastern Europe. So do pumpernickel and rye bread, with or without caraway seeds. Nobody knows who invented the bagel, that doughnut-shaped hard roll which gets its special texture from the fact that it is boiled before being baked. In this country bagel-and-lox has become a popular combination. Lox is smoked salmon. All kinds of fish — salted, pickled, and smoked — appear in Jewish delicatessens. The word delicatessen itself is German, though it comes from the French word, *delicatesse*.

Jewish delicatessens sell kosher corned beef, pastrami (spiced beef), salami, and other prepared meats. In Jewish neighborhoods there are also butcher shops with the word *kosher* on their signs. This means that the meats have been prepared according to *kashruth*, the Jewish dietary code. This code which comes from a Mosaic law forbids the eating of pork, which is called *treif* — meaning forbidden. All other domestic animals and poultry are eaten, but they have to be slaughtered in a prescribed way by a man trained for this job, who is called a *shochet*. Some parts of cattle, like the hind legs, are not eaten, but liver and tongue are kosher. Shellfish, incidentally, are not kosher. In addition, an old Biblical injunction not to "seethe a kid in its mother's milk" was construed to mean that milk or milk products, such as cheese and butter, should not be eaten with meat.

Limited as they were by these rules, Jewish cooks had to use considerable ingenuity in preparing their food. Since many of them had to be frugal as well, they used the materials that were cheap and plentiful, such as dried beans, peas, lentils, root vegetables, and dried fruits. A dish made of meat with carrots, or meat with potatoes and prunes, is called a *tsimess*. Cooks experimented with this dish by adding various ingredients and flavorings, and the word *tsimess* became part of a slang phrase. When someone wanted to say, "Don't exaggerate," or "Don't make a mountain out of a molehill," he said, "Don't make a whole tsimess out of it."

The Jewish holidays all have their special foods. Passover celebrates the escape from Egyptian bondage. Since the fleeing Israelites had no time to wait for their bread to rise, they ate flat cakes of unleavened bread. This is the *matzo* which is eaten instead of bread during the days of Passover. At the *seder* or Passover supper, a plate with symbolic foods is placed on the table. It contains horseradish to symbolize the bitter days of bondage, *charoseth,* a mixture of chopped apples, nuts, and wine, for the mortar which went toward the building of the pyramids, a bone of the Paschal lamb, and a sprig of parsley or other green vegetable to denote hope and the coming of spring.

For a reading on **Religion** *see page 121.*

Purim celebrates the feast of Queen Esther and the downfall of Haman, the enemy of the Jews. Cookies filled with prunes or poppyseed and shaped like triangles to represent Haman's hat are called *hamantashen.* And on Friday night, which ushers in the Sabbath, there is the large braided loaf of white bread, the *challah,* a bottle of wine, and that other traditional dish, gefilte fish, a type of fishball, usually accompanied by red or white horseradish.

75

The seder table, Passover.

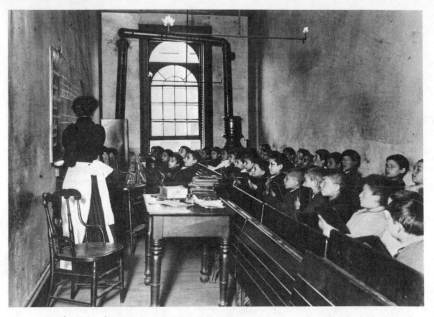

A class in the condemned Essex Market School, New York City. Photograph by Jacob A. Riis, about 1890.

The American Experience: Twentieth Century

1. *Transition*

For a reading on
Community
see page 113.

We have seen how the Jews in early America and those who came in the nineteenth century from Central Europe and Germany had adapted themselves to the American environment. Their descendants, feeling their own position to be secure, looked upon the masses of East European Jews pouring into the country with apprehension mingled with pity. The words inscribed on the pedestal of the Statue of Liberty applied to all immigrants, but they had been originally inspired by the plight of the East European Jews. America had indeed opened her "golden door," but would she be able to absorb these "huddled masses yearning to breathe free/The wretched refuse of your teeming shore"?

For a reading on
Identity
see page 109.

In the large cities welfare organizations formed by Jews of German descent and settlement houses built in slum areas worked hard to "Americanize" and "civilize" the immigrants. Often welfare workers making their rounds found to their surprise that the people they were trying to civilize had a rich and meaningful culture of their own and were quick to adopt American culture as well.

For a reading on *Integration* see page 138.

This was especially true of the children of immigrants. When a family arrived from Europe, the older children often had to work to help support the family, while the younger children went to public school. Both at work and in school the children learned the new language and new customs fast. Too fast, it seemed to their parents. They played in the street with other children (often of Italian or Irish descent), picked up American slang, adopted a whole new folklore, incomprehensible to their parents. In Hebrew school the children had been taught to admire the heroes of Jewish history — the Maccabees and Bar Kochba. Now they had a whole new set of heroes — prize-fighters and baseball players. In the synagogue they chanted the sacred music; in the street they picked up the tunes of Tin Pan Alley and American jazz. It could hardly be otherwise, for in the early years of the century what we now call "popular" American culture had its beginnings. To this popular culture many Jews made a significant contribution.

For a reading on *Integration* see page 138.

77

Playing under a street sprinkler. New York City, 1915.

Mordecai Kaplan has been a profound influence on the American Jewish scene. Developing his belief in "Judaism as an evolving religious civilization," he has founded the Jewish Reconstructionist Foundation and the Society for the Advancement of Judaism. He is also known for originating the "Jewish Center," and as a pioneer in the adoption of the *Bat Mitzvah* ceremony.

For a reading on
Identity
see page 110.

In 1911 "Alexander's Ragtime Band" was all the rage. It had been written and composed by Irving Berlin, who was born in Russia in 1888 and came to New York with his family as a small child. His father was a part-time cantor in a synagogue, his olders brothers worked in sweatshops and sold newspapers. At the age of nine after his father's death, Irving Berlin left home and earned his keep by leading a blind singer around the saloons on the Bowery. Later he became a singing waiter (like Eddie Cantor) and began composing songs for musical revues and plays, among them *Annie Get Your Gun* and *Call Me Madam.*

For a reading on
Education
see page 133.

Education had always been important to the Jews, both for its own sake and as a means of advancement. As the economic lot of the immigrants improved, their children stayed in school longer, and went on to high school and college. Even before World War I the sons and daughters of East European Jews were beginning to enter white collar and professional fields. And even the most old-fashioned parents wouldn't think of choosing a husband for a daughter who was out in the world, earning her living as a typist or schoolteacher.

At the same time, the dividing line which had once been sharply drawn between the Jews from Germany and those from Eastern Europe began to blur, and eventually disappeared. In a country where most people are of mixed national origins and where an aristocracy in the European sense doesn't exist, it matters little after a while if one's grandfather had been a shoemaker in Kovno, one's great-grandfather a merchant in Frankfurt, or one's many-times great-grandfather a physician in Cordoba.

SPORTS

Young Jews who wanted to make a living with their fists or pitching arms found wide opportunities in the early years of the century. Jewish athletes leaned particularly to boxing and baseball, two sports that required little money and no social status to undertake. Kid Kaplan and Benny Leonard, the lightweight champion from 1917 to 1924, were two of the world's best boxers in that or any era. Barney Ross, a champ in two divisions, fought and beat all comers in the 1930's, and in World War II battled his way to an equally distinguished combat record. Many Jewish baseball players made the big leagues in the 1920's and 1930's. The best was Hank Greenberg, who learned to hit on the streets of the Bronx. Greenberg, now a baseball executive, hit 58 homers in 1938, just two short of Babe Ruth's magic 60. Al (Flip) Rosen of the Cleveland Indians was the best known Jewish ballplayer of the 1950's, and Sandy Koufax, a Brooklyn boy, was the most feared pitcher in all of baseball during the 1960's. Jews excelled in other sports too. In basketball there was Nat Holman, the great player and coach. In football Benny Friedman of Michigan and Sid Luckman of Columbia College and the Chicago Bears were elected to the College Football Hall of Fame.

Hank Greenberg played first base for the Detroit Tigers from 1933 to 1946.

Sandy Koufax pitched for the Brooklyn and Los Angeles Dodgers from 1955 to 1966.

2. Setbacks

End of Immigration

For 300 years America had maintained an open-door policy toward European immigration. When 16 million people arrived from Europe within three or four decades, this policy began to be questioned. Labor objected on the ground that the immigrants threatened their jobs. The white-collar urban people had a vision of the cities being filled with slums. Farmers and small-town people in the West and South heard demagogues who assured them that pure white Anglo-Saxon America was being swallowed up by the "inferior" people from Southern and Eastern Europe. After the 1917 Russian Revolution, a hysteria swept the country, and every immigrant was suspected of carrying a bomb in his pocket. The United States Congress began passing anti-immigration acts culminating in the 1924 Johnson Bill which provided that only 2% of each nationality group be admitted each year. This percentage was based on the 1890 census when the large immigration waves had barely started. It practically put a stop to immigration from Southern and Eastern Europe. What Congress was saying, in effect, was that Italians, Slavs, and Jews were less desirable as citizens than the people of Northern Europe. This theory ran counter to the principles on which America had been founded. It aggravated many prejudices which already existed.

For a reading on **Israel** see page 147.

Anti-Semitism

For a reading on **Anti-Semitism** see page 144.

We have spoken earlier of the medieval myth of the Jew. This myth had to a large extent died out in modern times. No reasonable person would believe, for instance, that the Jews had caused the influenza epidemic of 1919 by poisoning the water system. But in 1911 many people were led to believe that a Jew in Russia, Mendel Beiliss, had killed a Christian child and used his blood for baking the Passover matzos. And at the turn of the century the Dreyfus case in France had rocked the world on both sides of the Atlantic. A parallel case in America was the Leo Frank case of 1915 in Atlanta, Georgia. Leo Frank, a Jew and a northerner, owned a factory in Atlanta. He had been charged on flimsy evidence of having killed a 14-year-old girl. He was sentenced to death, but his case aroused so much indignation all over the country, that the governor commuted the death sentence to imprisonment. Incensed by this commutation of the death sentence, a mob dragged Leo Frank out of prison and lynched him in Marietta, Georgia.

Social Justice, October 3, 1938. Father Coughlin's paper was barred from the mails for violation of the Espionage Act and ceased publication in 1942.

Modern anti-Semitism was fed from many sources. In the late nineteenth and early twentieth century books were written on both sides of the Atlantic setting forth the theory of the superiority of Aryan or Nordic races. In the American Middle West in the 1890's a movement called Populism arose among the farmers who were crying out for agrarian reforms. The Populists had a genuine grievance, but they believed that a conspiracy had been hatched against them in the big cities — New York and London — by "Jewish and English bankers." Their standard-bearer and hero was William Jennings Bryan, who in the 1896 election campaign made his famous "Cross of Gold" speech. This speech seemed to invoke an ancient image which linked the crucifixion and betrayal of Christ with the betrayal of the farmer by the "gold" or big money interests. The fact that at the time millions of Jews in this country were literally "Jews without money" had little influence on the popular mind.

In the 1920's anti-Semitism took on a more concrete form. Henry Ford published in his paper, *The Dearborn Independent,* a series of articles under the title of "The International Jew." These were supposed to be a transcript of a document known as "The Protocols of the Elders of Zion." This document had a curious history. It had first been "discovered" and publicized at the turn of the century in Russia by the Czar's secret police. It was supposed to be the transactions of a group called "The Elders of Zion," who had met in Prague and had plotted to take over the governments of the world with the help of corrupt politicians, Freemasons, liberals, and atheists. There

For a reading on *𝒜nti-Semitism* *see page 144.*

Father Charles Coughlin was pastor of
the Shrine of the Little Flower at Royal
Oak, Michigan, from 1926 until 1966.
During the 1930's his radio sermons be-
came increasingly political and anti-
Semitic.

had never been such a group or such a conspiracy. The document was
declared to be a forgery by several courts, in America and then in
Switzerland where it was used in 1935 by Nazi agents. Henry Ford
had to disclaim it at last; it was revived briefly by the Ku Klux Klan
and again discredited. But like all forgeries or daring libels, it left
an aura of ugly suspicion.

Between 1920 and 1930 the Ku Klux Klan, which began in the
reconstruction days after the Civil War, was revived and this time
the Klan attacked Negroes, Catholics, and Jews. In the 1930's after
the stock market crash had brought on a severe economic depression,
various crackpot organizations and individuals came forward. Father
Coughlin, a Catholic priest, in his newspaper *Social Justice* and in
weekly radio broadcasts blamed the ills of society on "international
Jewish bankers and radicals." He was eventually silenced by the
Church itself.

In those years discrimination was practiced against Jews in housing
and employment. Many companies made no secret of the fact that
they didn't hire Jews. Certain neighborhoods were restricted to Jews
who wanted to rent or buy homes. Many universities and colleges
adopted a quota system which limited the number of Jewish students
to a certain percentage.

Hitler's rise to power in Germany and his attacks against the Jews
had their echoes in America. The German-American Bund with Fritz
Kuhn at its head held meetings that were a replica on a smaller scale

Supreme Court justices **Louis D. Brandeis** (1856-1941) and **Benjamin Cardozo** (1870-1938) were liberal jurists who based their interpretation of law upon social change. Brandeis served on the Court from 1916 to 1939, Cardozo from 1932 to 1938.

of anti-Jewish meetings in Nazi Germany. Local hate groups sprang up as well, such as William Dudley Pelley's Silver Shirts, which patterned itself on the fascist Black Shirts and the Nazi Brown Shirts. They made speeches, circulated anti-Semitic books and pamphlets, and looked to their local "fuehrers" to start a real assault on the Jews. When President Roosevelt initiated The New Deal he was attacked by these hate groups as well as by his political opponents, who made much of the fact that some of his advisers, or Brain Trust, happened to be Jews. Some of the more abusive attacks on the President had anti-Semitic overtones.

Justice **Felix Frankfurter** (1882-1965), born in Vienna, came to the United States in 1894. He was a professor of law at Harvard when Franklin Roosevelt appointed him to the Court in 1939. Frankfurter retired in 1962. Since then, Arthur Goldberg and Abe Fortas have served on the Court.

83

For a reading on
Anti-Semitism
see page 145.

The attack on Pearl Harbor and the declaration of war on Nazi Germany dispersed the local Nazi groups and dealt a most effective blow against organized anti-Semitism. Jews in all walks of life fought in the war along with Americans of every national origin — including German and Japanese. When the war ended in 1945 and the enormity of what Hitler had done to the Jews of Germany and the German-occupied countries became known, a feeling of revulsion against Nazi ideas and methods turned the tide of anti-Semitism. Six million Jews had been killed or exterminated in Nazi death camps. The realization that anti-Semitism could be carried to such a conclusion in modern times shocked the American people. Political as well as Jewish exiles

For a reading on
Anti-Semitism
see page 146.

from Germany and Eastern Europe had come to the United States before the war. Under the Displaced Persons Act of 1948, 72,000 Jews were admitted after the war. Among them were scientists, scholars, and artists, as well as people of other skills who had been able to survive the concentration camps. For the most part they found America to be the refuge she had been since the day old Peter Stuyvesant agreed to allow the first 23 Jews to land in New Amsterdam.

After the Germans took Warsaw in 1939, they packed 500,000 Jews into a walled ghetto within the Jewish quarter of the city. In 1942-43 (above) large numbers were deported to death camps. A ghetto uprising broke out on April 19, 1943. It ended a month later when Germans demolished the ghetto.

Jewish Population of American Cities

New York City	1,836,000
Los Angeles	490,000*
Philadelphia	330,000*
Chicago	290,000
Boston	169,000*
Newark	100,000
Miami	92,000
Washington, D. C.	90,000*
Baltimore	85,000
Cleveland	85,000
Detroit	85,000
San Francisco	71,000*
St. Louis	57,000

*greater area

(Estimated 1967 figures, Jewish Statistical Bureau)

3. Statistics

Out of an estimated 13 million Jews in the world today, 5.7 million live in the United States. If we looked at the distribution of the remaining 7.3 million, we would see that the United States has the largest number of Jews of any country in the world. In a total population of 195 million their percentage is 2.9%. This is not a large percentage — less than 3 out of 100; but with the exception of Israel, this is the largest percentage of any country in the world.

For a reading on *Israel* see page 148.

The reasons for the dramatic shift of Jewish population from Europe to America are not hard to find. The first is the large waves of immigration that took place in the nineteenth and early twentieth centuries. The second is the destruction of European Jews by the Nazis prior to and including World War II. The third reason lies in the nature of the American experience. For the first time in the long history of their wanderings the Jews found a country in which they did not have to court the favor of kings and autocratic governments. In America they could live as free individuals and not as a people apart. At the same time they have not had to submerge their identity or to give up their cultural heritage. Indeed this heritage, part of which was handed down from ancient times and part of which they acquired in the various lands of the diaspora, or exile, has played an important part in shaping American culture.

For a reading on *Integration* see page 139.

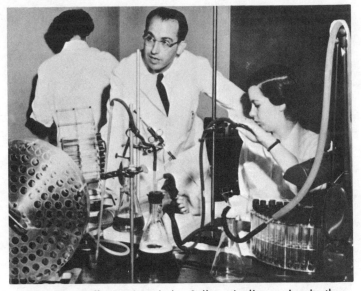

Dr. Jonas Salk developed the Salk antipolio vaccine in the Virus Research Laboratory at the University of Pittsburgh. Here, Salk inspects the work of a research assistant as she draws fluid from culture tubes.

4. *Science*

From the earliest times the Jews have valued the art of healing. Before medicine became the science it is today, there were Jewish doctors at the courts of kings, and two of the Marranos with Columbus were doctors. Today there are Jewish doctors in every branch of medical practice, on the teaching staffs of medical colleges, and in research laboratories throughout the country. In medicine the names of diseases or their cures are often associated with the names of the scientists who have discovered these diseases or their cures. Salk polio vaccine is named for Dr. Jonas Salk who developed the first vaccine which gives 98% immunity to paralytic poliomyelitis. Flexner B Dysentery was named for Dr. Simon Flexner of the Rockefeller Foundation who isolated the bacillus of that disease in 1889. He also made experimental studies of diphtheria toxins and is noted for discovery of serum treatment of spinal meningitis.

A Jewish doctor who pioneered in preventive medicine was Joseph Goldberger (1874-1929). He was born in Austria and brought to this country at the age of six. He graduated from Bellevue Hospital Medical

School in New York. In 1899 he entered the U.S. Public Health Service and was sent to Cuba and Mexico where he studied yellow fever and typhus, often using himself as a guinea pig. Between 1913 and 1925 he made a study of pellagra among the poor whites and Negroes in the South. It was thought at that time that pellagra was caused by a disease germ. Dr. Goldberger demonstrated that this disease was caused by the poor diet of the people of the South. His findings laid the basis for the modern science of nutrition.

Dr. Selman A. Waksman, working with a team of research scientists in soil chemistry at the New Jersey Agricultural Experiment Station, isolated streptomycin, the second antibiotic, the first being penicillin. It was he who named this and similar substances *antibiotics*. Streptomycin is effective against many diseases, but especially against tuberculosis. Its use has revolutionized the treatment of that once almost fatal disease. For this discovery and for subsequent work with other antibiotics Dr. Waksman received the Nobel Prize in Physiology and Medicine in 1952.

In 1921 the Nobel Prize for Physics was awarded to Albert Einstein. Einstein, whose theory of relativity is considered the greatest single scientific discovery of modern times, was a German Jew, but he had gone to Switzerland as a young man and did most of his important scientific work there. In 1934 he came to America to head the school of mathematics in the Institute for Advanced Study at Princeton, New Jersey, where he taught and worked until his death.

Selman Waksman, professor emeritus of microbiology at Rutgers University.

Another Nobel Prize winner in Physics (1944) was I. I. Rabi who received the prize for his work in phenomena connected directly or indirectly with magnetic fields. Isador Isaac Rabi was born in Austria in 1898 and was brought to the United States as a child. He graduated from Cornell University and received his Ph.D. from Columbia University in 1927. He has been associated with Columbia University ever since, becoming in 1964 the first man with the title of University Professor, a professorship without departmental ties. During World War II he did research in the field of microwave radar. From 1946 to 1956 he was a member of the General Advisory Committee of the Atomic Energy Commission. He has done valuable research on the peaceful uses of atomic energy and originated the movement resulting in CERN at Geneva, an international laboratory for the study of high energy physics.

A number of American Jewish physicists have made a contribution to the study of atomic energy and to the development of the first atom bomb. The most prominent among them was J. Robert Oppenheimer, who directed the Los Alamos laboratory where the first atom bomb was developed.

Albert Einstein (1879-1955) came to America in 1934. He had been director of theoretical physics at the Kaiser Wilhelm Institute in Berlin from 1914 until 1933, when the Nazis took away his property, his position, and his German citizenship.

Robert Oppenheimer (1904-1967) was a great teacher as well as a noted physicist.

Oppenheimer was born in New York in 1904, the son of a textile manufacturer who had come from Germany in 1888. He graduated from Harvard in 1926, and later studied at Cambridge University, England, and Gottingen, Germany. Between 1929 and 1947 he taught at the University of California and at Cal Tech and did research in theoretical physics. His interests extended beyond science to literature and the arts, but he did not become interested in economics and politics until about 1936. Then the events in Nazi Germany — Hitler's persecution of Jews — and the depression in this country (which made it hard for many of his students to find jobs) deeply disturbed him. During this period many intellectuals, scientists, and artists were also disturbed and took part in left-wing political movements. Though Oppenheimer did not join any political party, he had friends who did, and for this "guilt by association" he was to suffer later.

Meanwhile Oppenheimer was doing research in atomic energy. In 1943 he was appointed director of the Los Alamos, New Mexico, laboratory and headed a team of scientists and technicians who succeeded in exploding the first atom bomb. After the war, from 1947 to 1952, he was chairman of the General Advisory Council of the Atomic Energy Commission. Along with several other scientists he refused to work on the hydrogen bomb.

In December 1953 the AEC decided to review his loyalty status. In April 1954 his case was reviewed and he was cleared of charges of disloyalty, but was not given complete security clearance and was not allowed to continue to work on the AEC. Oppenheimer, who was director of the Institute for Advanced Study at Princeton, worked there until shortly before his death in 1967. In December 1963 Oppenheimer's contributions to science were acknowledged, and at the same time some restitution was made to him for the slur of the decade before, when he received the Fermi Award of $50,000, the Atomic Energy Commission's highest public award.

GOVERNMENT

During the presidency of Franklin Roosevelt, a number of administrative and advisory positions were held by Jews. Roosevelt's friend and neighbor from New York State, Henry Morgenthau, Jr., served as Secretary of the Treasury. Morgenthau initiated the successful wartime drive for Victory Bonds and was an advocate of worldwide monetary reform. David Lilienthal was a director and chairman of the Tennessee Valley Authority and in 1947 became the first chairman of the Atomic Energy Commission. Anna Rosenberg, an expert in labor and personnel relations, held positions with several government agencies during the New Deal years, and was Assistant Secretary of Defense in the Truman administration, from 1950 to 1953. Financier Bernard Baruch acted as an advisor on economics and national defense to every President from Woodrow Wilson to John F. Kennedy.

In 1932, Democrat Herbert Lehman followed Franklin Roosevelt as governor of New York. He served until 1942, and in 1949 was elected to the United States Senate. Lehman remained active in politics after his retirement in 1956, leading a reform movement within the Democratic party of New York City. Another Democrat, Ernest Gruening, was appointed governor of the Alaska territory in 1939. He campaigned for statehood and served as one of Alaska's first Senators, from 1959 to 1968. Richard Neuberger of Oregon was a member of the Senate from 1955 until his death in 1960, when his wife Maurine was elected to his seat. The Neubergers' special interests were conservation, health, and consumer protection. In 1961 President Kennedy appointed Governor Abraham Ribicoff of Connecticut to his Cabinet, as Secretary of Health, Education, and Welfare. Ribicoff was elected to the United States Senate in 1962. Jacob Javits of New York, a leader among liberal Republicans, entered the Senate in 1957 and was elected to a third term in 1968.

A noted Chicago labor lawyer, Arthur Goldberg, was Secretary of Labor under President Kennedy. He became an associate justice of the Supreme Court in 1962 and was ambassador to the United Nations from 1965 until 1968.

5. *Business and Industry*

American Jews have been prominent in two industries (besides the retailing and garment industries already mentioned) — publishing and entertainment. There is still a Yiddish language press, though its reading public has dwindled. Several book publishers specialize in Yiddish and Hebrew books as well as English language books oriented toward the Jewish reader. The oldest of these is the Bloch Publishing Company, founded in 1854 in Cincinnati by Edward Bloch and Rabbi Isaac Wise. From Cincinnati it moved to Chicago, and then to New York. The Jewish Publication Society, established in Philadelphia in 1888, succeeded an earlier company founded in 1854.

For a reading on *Education* see page 133.

In the last 30 or 40 years, however, Jews have entered in great numbers into the general American publishing field. Among them, Alfred Knopf is distinguished especially in publishing foreign authors in this country.

In the late nineteenth century several newspapers were rescued and given new life by two noted publishers. Joseph Pulitzer (1847-1911), half-Jewish, came to America from Hungary in 1864. He combined two papers to form the *St. Louis Post-Dispatch,* then moved on to the *New York World.* Before his death he established a school of journalism at Columbia University and endowed the Pulitzer prizes which have been awarded since 1917. His family still publishes the *Post-Dispatch.* In 1896 Adolph Ochs (1858-1935) went to New York from Chattanooga, Tennessee; he became the publisher of *The New York Times,* then on the verge of bankruptcy, and developed it into one of the world's greatest newspapers.

In the American theatre, a succession of notable producers has followed David Belasco's work at the turn of the century: Lee Shubert, Jed Harris, Herman Shumlin, and others. Shubert and his brothers managed and built theatres, staged operettas, and originated the modern musical revue. Shubert Alley remains a familiar spot in the New York theatre district.

Jews were pioneers in the movie industry. Adolph Zukor's career began in a penny arcade in 1903. Impressed by the popularity of imported French films, he formed his own company, Famous Players, and produced some of the earliest multi-reel feature length films. As an independent producer, he was given financial backing by Paramount Pictures, and later became president of Paramount. The four Warner

David Belasco (1853-1931), an innovator in the American theatre, came from San Francisco to New York as a stage manager in 1882 and by 1895 was guiding his own productions. Belasco wrote and directed plays, picked stars, designed sets. A master of elaborate stage effects, he specialized in storms.

brothers began making films in the early twenties. Public interest in movies was waning by the mid-twenties and the Warners made a desperate move to win back audiences. *Don Juan* in 1926 had a musical sound track, and in 1927 they released *The Jazz Singer,* considered to be the first talking picture, though it had little audible dialogue beyond the songs of Al Jolson. In July 1928 another Warner film, *The Lights of New York,* was the first full-dialogue release.

A series of mergers led to the formation of Metro-Goldwyn-Mayer in 1924. The Goldwyn and Metro companies had combined and were on the verge of bankruptcy when they joined forces with producers Louis B. Mayer and Irving Thalberg. Mayer, who had once been a scrap merchant, became one of Hollywood's flamboyant tycoons, and eventually headed the M-G-M company. Thalberg's career was short but brilliant. He had grown up in Brooklyn, and entered the film industry as a young secretary in the New York offices of Universal Pictures. His boss, Carl Laemmle, took him to Hollywood, where he learned production and rose quickly, hence was known as a "boy wonder." Sensitive to public taste, Thalberg was a hard-working producer who took part in every aspect of film-making. During the thirties some of his best films were *The Barretts of Wimpole Street* (with his wife Norma Shearer in the role of Elizabeth Barrett), *Mutiny on the Bounty,* and *Romeo and Juliet.* He died in 1936 at the age 37. F. Scott Fitzgerald drew upon the personality and career of Thalberg when he wrote *The Last Tycoon,* a novel which Fitzgerald himself did not live to finish.

6. Theatre and Films

Theatre has two masks—tragedy and comedy. So many Jewish American actors and actresses have donned the mask of comedy that they are sometimes credited with having a corner on that branch of entertainment. This isn't quite true, of course. Comedy on the American stage has drawn heavily on the various ethnic groups—Irish, Italians, and others. The Jews have only contributed their share. From the zany antics of the four Marx brothers in the early films to the deadpan humor of Jack Benny, from the comic impersonations of Sid Caesar in the early days of television to the trenchant wit of Mort Sahl and other stand-up comedians, they have made several generations of American audiences laugh, chuckle or smile.

Danny Kaye is a comic genius in the great tradition. He was born in 1913 in Brooklyn, New York, as David Daniel Kaminsky, the son of a tailor. His first performance is supposed to have been in a school play and the part he played was that of a watermelon seed. At 13 he joined the "Borscht circuit," a name given to the summer resorts in the Catskill Mountains which catered mainly to Jewish audiences from New York and the vicinity. From there he went on to a successful career on stage, screen, and television. His wife Sylvia Fine has written most of his acts.

Brooklyn was also the birthplace of Zero Mostel (Samuel Joseph Mostel) who was born in 1915. His father was a rabbi. Where did he find the name Zero? He hit upon it "from nothing," it is reported. He is both a comedian and a character actor. His plays have been *A Funny Thing Happened on the Way to the Forum, Rhinoceros,* and *Waiting for Godot.* He created the part of Tevye in the musical *Fiddler on the Roof.*

The Marx brothers: Groucho, Harpo, and Chico.

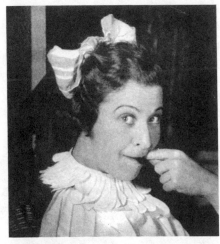

Fanny Brice (1891-1951), a New Yorker, got her first big break in the Ziegfield Follies of 1910. A comic, singer, and mimic, she appeared in revues through the 1930's. Radio audiences knew her as Baby Snooks (above).

Brooklyn-born actor **Eli Wallach** co-starred with Zero Mostel in *Rhinoceros*, and with his wife Anne Jackson in *The Typists* and *The Tiger* (1963) and *Luv* (1964).

Among **Danny Kaye's** best films are *The Secret Life of Walter Mitty, The Inspector General,* and *Me and the Colonel.* He has entertained children all over the world for UNICEF.

Zero Mostel appeared in the stage and screen versions of *A Funny Thing Happened on the Way to the Forum.*

Judy Holliday won an Academy Award in 1950 for *Born Yesterday*, recreating a role she had originated on Broadway. She made the gum-chewing blond, Billie Dawn, not only funny but also human and moving, according to an article in the *New York Times* at the time of her death in 1965. Her acting career had started at the Village Vanguard with a group called the Revuers which included Adolph Green and Betty Comden. Comden and Green later wrote the play *Bells Are Ringing* which starred Judy Holliday in both stage and screen productions.

Another Oscar-winner, Shelley Winters, was named best supporting actress of 1959 for the part of Mrs. Van Daan in *The Diary of Anne Frank*. Actors Lee J. Cobb and Howard da Silva have had long careers on stage and in films and television. Cobb created the role of Willie Loman in Arthur Miller's *Death of a Salesman*. Da Silva, who directed and appeared in *The World of Sholom Aleichem* (1953) is perhaps best known for his roles in *Oklahoma!* and *Fiorello!* Most audiences are familiar with the work of Edward G. Robinson and Kirk Douglas, as well as with a new generation of performers — Barbra Streisand, actor-director Mike Nichols, Elaine May, George Segal, and singers Bob Dylan and Simon and Garfunkel.

7. *Music*

There is a story by Sholom Aleichem called "The Fiddle" about a boy who passionately loves music and wants above all else in the world to learn to play the fiddle. He knows that his prosperous, respectable father would never allow this, because to his father musicians are a ragged, disreputable lot who scrape away on their instruments at weddings and in country taverns. The boy goes to the sod-roofed hut of one of these village musicians and arranges to get fiddle lessons in secret. He is treated to a concert by the family orchestra of ragamuffins who play every kind of instrument including some home-made ones. The boy is also treated to a long and involved lecture "on music in general and fiddle-playing in particular" by the orchestra leader, a man named Naftalzi Bezborodka (*Bezborodka* means beardless). Carried away by his own eloquence, the village fiddler concludes, "The first fiddler in the world was Tubal Cain or Methuselah, I am not sure which.... The second fiddler was King David. The third, a man named Paganini, also a Jew. The best fiddlers have always been Jews."

Pianist **Artur Rubinstein,** born in Poland in 1887, is considered one of the finest interpreters of Chopin.

A comic and touching boast, it was intended as irony in the context of the story. But this boast had a curiously prophetic ring. In the "lost" villages of the Russian Pale, during the latter part of the nineteenth century, village fiddlers were looked down upon, and boys like the hero of this story had to give up their dream of learning the fiddle. But in the next generation young people with musical talent were to be trained in the finest Russian conservatories and were to emerge as the great violin virtuosos of our time. Among them were Mischa Elman, Jascha Heifetz, and Nathan Milstein, all of whom later adopted America as their country. There were also pianists, and conductors. Still later came the American-born generation of Jewish musicians, singers, and composers of theatre music.

From *Watch Your Step* to *On Your Toes* and *Lady Be Good!* to *My Fair Lady,* the work of American Jewish composers and lyricists has run the full range of twentieth-century musical theatre. Critics and historians consider the musical comedy a distinctive American art form and trace its development from the operetta, variety show, and revue; they note the gradual integration of song and story, as well as the influence of jazz in the twenties and ballet in the thirties. Songs from the musical theatre form a kind of track through the American mind: the best songs catch the tone (or set the tone) of the year, and continue to be sung, whistled, even recorded long after the plays have closed. Irving Berlin, Jerome Kern, George Gershwin, Richard Rodgers

96

Jascha Heifetz, born in Lithuania in 1901, studied with his father before entering the St. Petersburg Conservatory in 1910. Unlike most child prodigies, he became even greater as an adult performer.

(with Lorenz Hart and Oscar Hammerstein), Frederick Loewe (with Alan Jay Lerner), and Leonard Bernstein are perhaps the best known of the Jewish composers for Broadway theatre.

One of the most haunting theatre songs, "Mack the Knife," is from an off-Broadway play, *The Threepenny Opera,* and is the result of an unusual collaboration. Its composer Kurt Weill came to America in 1935, two years after leaving Nazi Germany. *Threepenny* (with text by German playwright Bertolt Brecht) had opened in 1928 at a small theatre in Berlin. It ran for five years and was popular throughout Europe during the thirties. Although it appeared briefly on Broadway

Tenors **Richard Tucker** (left) and **Jan Peerce.** Tucker was a cantor at the Brooklyn Jewish Center before his debut with the Metropolitan Opera in 1945. Peerce first appeared at the Met in 1941, as Alfredo in *La Traviata.*

George Gershwin (1898-1937) first played *Rhapsody in Blue* with Paul Whiteman's orchestra in 1924—the same year that *Lady Be Good!* opened on Broadway. His use of jazz rhythms marked a turning point in American music. Most of Gershwin's lyrics were written by his brother Ira.

in 1933, nearly 20 years were to pass before American audiences would see an effective English version of the play.

Weill remained in America for the rest of his life, and composed a number of fine scores for the American musical theatre—*Knickerbocker Holiday, Lady in the Dark, Lost in the Stars*. In 1950 Marc Blitzstein showed him a translation he had made of one of the songs from *Threepenny*, which he had seen as a student in Germany. After Weill's death, Blitzstein, a notable composer and lyricist in his own right, went ahead and made a brilliant adaptation of the text and the remaining songs. *Threepenny Opera* began its long off-Broadway run in March 1954. Since then it has also been staged by many civic theatres and colleges.

Leonard Bernstein, music director of the New York Philharmonic from 1958 to 1969, was the first American-born and -trained conductor to hold that post. A pianist, teacher, and composer, Bernstein's scores include *On the Town, Wonderful Town,* and *West Side Story*.

Sculptor **Seymour Lipton** works chiefly in sheet metal with textured overlays of molten bronze. His pieces combine mechanical and natural forms.

8. *Art*

In 1905 a young American artist named Max Weber arrived in Paris. This was a momentous year in the history of art, for in that year Cezanne, Matisse, and other modern French painters, who had been turned down by the staid French Academy of Art, held their first public exhibitions at the now famous Autumn Salon. Weber remained in Paris for three years and studied with Henri Matisse. When he returned to America he brought with him the concepts and techniques in painting which were considered revolutionary at the time, but which have since become accepted and have influenced modern art, both abstract and representational.

Max Weber (1881-1961) was the son of Russian-Jewish immigrant parents who had come to America when he was 10 years old. Like most immigrants, his family was poor, but he managed to study art at the Pratt Institute in Brooklyn before going to Paris. In his early paintings based on New York scenes he demonstrated a free and dynamic use of form and color. His painting *Chinese Restaurant* (1915), owned by the Whitney Museum of American Art, is often reproduced as an example of American abstract art. Later in his career Weber's work became representational and he turned for subjects to his

Jewish background. Examples of this work are *The Hasidic Dance* and *Adoration of the Moon.* The latter is derived from an old Jewish ceremony in which 10 men at the close of the Sabbath gather in the courtyard of the synagogue to bless the rising moon when its light is the strongest.

Mark Rothko (1903-1970), an abstract painter, was at one time a student of Weber's. Rothko was born in Russia and grew up in Oregon. His paintings hang in the Whitney, the Museum of Modern Art, and the Chicago Art Institute.

Emphatic in his opposition to abstract art, Aaron Bohrod derives from the regional school of American painters. Born and raised in Chicago, he has said that he wanted to do for Chicago what John Sloan had done for New York—that is, paint city streets, houses, railroads—whether they were conventionally beautiful or not. He has done this with success. Appointed artist in residence at the University of Wisconsin he has painted the towns and countryside of the Middle West, as well as scenes from the West and South. In recent years he has done striking still life paintings, and worked on pottery and textile design.

Represented at the Whitney, the Museum of Modern Art, and other leading American art galleries are Hyman Bloom and Jack Levine, both of Boston. Expressionist in technique, their paintings are rich in texture, brilliant in color. Bloom has used Jewish subjects of cantors,

Alfred Stieglitz (1864-1946), photographer and art dealer, opened the Photo-Secession Gallery at 291 Fifth Avenue in 1906. At "291" Stieglitz exhibited for the first time in America the work of Matisse and other modern French and American painters.

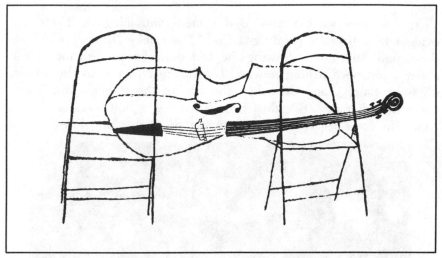

Cello With Chairs, a drawing by Ben Shahn.

rabbis, synagogue interiors. Jack Levine's paintings are satiric in subject matter, close to caricature. He paints groups of people to illustrate avarice, greed, and violence in modern society. Two examples often reproduced are *Gangster's Funeral* (1952) and *Military Symphony* (1962).

Ben Shahn (1898-1969) was an artist of remarkable range and versatility, whose work included fresco murals, oil paintings, and water colors, as well as posters and book and magazine illustrations. The son of a carpenter, he was born in Russia and was brought to New York at the age of eight. As a young boy in Brooklyn playing with neighborhood kids he did sidewalk chalk drawings of the sports heroes of the day. He attended high school at night and worked during the day as a lithographer's apprentice. His work as a lithographer gave him a thorough knowledge of draughtmanship and a respect for art as a *craft*. One of the first books he illustrated was a *Haggadah,* the Hebrew book of the Passover service. In the 1930's and 1940's he, along with many artists, worked for the Federal Arts Project. He made fresco murals for government buildings — the Bronx Central Annex Post Office, the Federal Security Building in Washington, and a housing development for garment workers in Roosevelt, New Jersey. This last mural is a series of panels depicting the history of American immigrants.

In his later work Shahn used symbol and allegory. These are evident in a group of paintings called "The Lucky Dragon" which he developed from some drawings he had done for a magazine article about a Japanese fishing trawler, *The Lucky Dragon*. In the article, physicist Ralph Lapp described the fate of the trawler, which was covered with radioactive dust from a hydrogen bomb test at Bikini Atoll. The crew became sick and one man died after long illness.

Wedding dance — a scene from the M-G-M film
The Fixer, based on Bernard Malamud's novel.

9. *Literature*

In 1966 two books came out almost simultaneously, one of them a novel, the other a historical account, on the same theme. The novel was *The Fixer* by Bernard Malamud; the historical account was *Blood Accusation: The Strange History of the Beiliss Case* by Maurice Samuel. Both of these books have been widely read and favorably received by the critics. That they should win praise for their literary merit is understandable. Bernard Malamud is one of the leading novelists writing in America today, while Maurice Samuel is a distinguished scholar and writer on subjects pertaining to Judaism. That the theme of these

Twenty years after publication of his World War II novel *The Naked and the Dead*, **Norman Mailer** wrote *The Armies of the Night*, a vivid account of the October 1967 march on the Pentagon to protest the war in Vietnam.

two books — the court trial of an obscure Jew in Czarist Russia over 50 years ago — should capture the interest of the American reading public is a cause for wonder. The wonder is dispelled when we realize the importance and growing popularity of Jewish subjects and of books with Jewish background in the world today. The Nobel Prize for literature in 1966 was shared by two Jewish writers, S. Y. Agnon of Israel and Nellie Sachs of Sweden. But it is chiefly in America that books of Jewish interest are being published and read at an astonishing rate. This has been true since the end of World War II, and even more so in the last 10 or 15 years.

Why is this true? One reason is that American Jewish writers have become intensely aware of their heritage and have been rediscovering their own background as a rich source of material. Yet all of these books have not been written by Jews. *The Wall*, a novel about the heroic uprising in the Warsaw ghetto in 1943, was written by John Hersey. *The Source*, a novel which covers the whole panorama of Jewish history, is by James Michener, who first became known for his *Tales of the South Pacific*. The Jew in literature is no longer an exotic character. Neither is he a stereotype. Earlier books about Jews, like *What Makes Sammy Run* (1941) and *I Can Get It For You Wholesale* (1937) caricatured the self-seeking ambitious Jew. By contrast, Herbert Gold's *Fathers* (1966) probes more deeply and with greater sympathy into the motivations of a man with ambition and drive to succeed.

For a reading on *Identity* see page 111.

Saul Bellow's novels and stories reflect his Jewish background and his understanding of the Jewish-American character. He received National Book Awards for *The Adventures of Augie March* (1953) and *Herzog* (1964) and is considered by many critics to be one of the foremost American writers of fiction.

In the short story, the character sketch, and the memoir, writers have captured the essence of growing up as the children of Jewish immigrants in America. Among these are Meyer Levin's *The Old Bunch,* Michael Gold's *Jews Without Money,* Charles Angoff's *When I Was a Boy in Boston,* Henry Roth's *Call It Sleep,* and Alfred Kazin's *A Walker in the City.* J. D. Salinger's stories about the Glass family have been especially interesting to young readers, and so has his novel, *Catcher in the Rye. The Diary of Anne Frank,* though European in origin, has become a small American classic.

Jewish writers have not confined themselves to Jewish subjects. Ben Hecht, Robert Nathan, Nathanael West, Dorothy Parker, and Edna Ferber have written on a variety of themes, ranging from fantasy to satire to historical romance. Two of the best World War II novels were written by American Jews — *The Young Lions* by Irwin Shaw and *The Naked and the Dead* by Norman Mailer. In his recent books Mailer has used his skill as a novelist to write about current history. There are many American Jewish literary critics of note — Lionel Trilling, Irving Howe, Philip Rahv, Leslie Fiedler. Some of these men also teach literature in universities and colleges.

In the 1920's the American theatre was enlivened by playwrights of Jewish origin — George Kaufman, Moss Hart, S. N. Behrman, Elmer Rice, Sidney Kingsley. During the 1930's Clifford Odets wrote plays of social protest. *Awake and Sing* was about a Jewish family caught in the depression, *Golden Boy* about an Italian youth forced by poverty to turn from music to professional prizefighting. Odets's plays were produced by the Group Theatre of which Harold Clurman was one of the founders and directors. Clurman is one of the best drama critics writing today.

Lillian Hellman, a native of New Orleans, became known for her play *The Children's Hour* in 1935. She is best known for *The Little Foxes,* a play about the changing South, which became a film and an opera (*Regina,* with music by Marc Blitzstein). Her *Watch on the Rhine* (1943), an anti-Nazi play, was revived in 1968.

One of the leading playwrights in America is Arthur Miller whose *Death of a Salesman,* first produced in 1949, has appeared throughout the world. His other plays include *All My Sons, The Crucible,* and *A View from the Bridge.* Miller has not dealt with Jewish characters or themes, but in *The Price* (1968) he introduced an old Jewish furniture dealer, a minor character who added depth and humor to the play.

A Jewish American writer of great power and originality, Edward Wallant, was born in New Haven, Connecticut, in 1926 and died in 1962 at the age of 36. He wrote four novels, two of which were published after his death. He wrote of submerged people, Jews and Italians in city ghettos. *The Pawnbroker* is about a Jew, Saul Nazerman, who

For a reading on
Justice
see page 128.

Isaac Bashevis Singer came to New York from Poland in 1935. His short stories and novels, all written in Yiddish, have been translated into English. *Zlateh the Goat,* his first children's book, is a collection of stories drawn from Jewish folklore.

had been a university professor in Poland, saw his wife and two children killed in a Nazi concentration camp, and then managed to escape to America. He became a pawnbroker in Harlem. The novel, and the film based on it, is a modern fable with terrifying implications. A man deprived of his humanity—of everything he cares for in life—turns into a lifeless automaton. He treats the derelicts and the poor who come to him—the Puerto Ricans and Negroes—with cruel indifference. When violence erupts and his young Puerto Rican assistant gets killed in trying to save him, the pawnbroker is at last able to feel pain. Though it is too late to undo the harm he has caused, he is a human being once more.

Awake and Sing! Act II, scene I from the Group Theatre production of Clifford Odets's play, 1935. Onstage (left to right): actors John Garfield, Morris Carnovsky, J. Edward Bromberg, Stella and Luther Adler, Sanford Meisner, and Art Smith. The title of the play is from lines spoken by the grandfather (Morris Carnovsky), quoting the prophet Isaiah: "Awake and sing, ye that dwell in dust, and the earth shall cast out the dead." *(Courtesy of the Theatre Collection, The New York Public Library at Lincoln Center)*

The Sources

Identity

Religious Freedom in the Public Schools (text, page 16)

A study of Jews in suburbia showed that Jewish families are concerned about Christian religious observances in the public schools. Parents complained that Jewish students are not always allowed to have their own beliefs and practices.

Jewish families express their concern about the scheduling of . . . sporting events on Jewish Festivals and Holy Days. Even more Jews are disturbed because Jewish Holy Days are so frequently ignored when examinations are scheduled in the . . . schools.

"It almost seems deliberate. The teachers . . . set examinations on a Jewish Holy Day . . . thereby making it impossible for our children to go to their synagogue and worship in peace. [If you object] you get such replies as 'Well, the Jewish festival is not on our calendar,' or, 'Teachers are autonomous. We cannot control each and everything they do,' or, 'How were we to know this was a Jewish holiday?' (even though the principal . . . received a Jewish calendar giving all the festival dates for a year ahead)."

The major source of tension . . . becomes evident around the Christmas-Chanukah season. . . parents are generally indignant about the manner in which Christmas has been incorporated in the public school programs, from kindergarten through high school. Preparation for the school Christmas program, emphasis upon gift-giving, discussion of the New Testament's record of the birth of Jesus, the carols [about Jesus] —all these are regarded as intrusions into the public school system [in violation of the] Constitutional guarantees of separation of church and state.

Jewish parents, often disturbed by this issue, react to this situation on different levels. Children are told that they . . . should not join in singing Christmas carols or participate in other activities directly associated with preparation for Christmas . . . Jewish children . . . sometimes ask for the right to introduce the theme of Chanukah, which usually occurs at the same season. To counteract the influence of the Christmas season upon their children, Jewish parents have converted this minor Jewish festival into [a major one. Through their organizations and] their congregational leaders, they carry on a [constant] campaign to root out . . . religious festivals from tax-supported public schools. (Gordon, Albert. *Jews in Suburbia.* Boston: Beacon Press, 1959.)

Emma Lazarus Realizes Her Jewish Identity (text, page 76)

Emma Lazarus was a young American poetess. She was at first uninterested in being Jewish. But news of the persecution of Jews in Eastern Europe so angered her, that she experienced a new self-awareness becoming a voice for the Jewish People. The following account is given by Anita Lebeson in *Recall to life.*

Like a delicate instrument attuned to record distant earthquakes, Emma reacted to distant atrocities to which her fellow Jews were subjected . . .

There was no turning back. Her frail self, her sheltered and protected inner being was pierced. This was to be her major preoccupation until early death came. Her identification with Jews was complete. Many were "the literary fruits" of this hour of truth. Contact with Russian Jewish refugees led her to the Bible, to Jewish history, to the study of Hebrew. Her sister writes: "All this time she had been seeking heroic ideals in alien stock, soulless and far removed . . . Hitherto Judiasm had been a dead letter to her . . ." It was a dead letter no longer. In "The Banner of the Jew" she rose to new heights. She was a prophet exhorting her people in language as majestic, as exalted, as ever the Prophets uttered:

Wake, Israel, wake! Recall today
The glorious Maccabean rage . . .
Oh, deem not dead that martial fire,
Say not the mystic flame is spent!
With Moses' law and David's lyre,
Your ancient strength remains unbent.
Let but an Ezra rise anew,
To lift the *Banner of the Jew!*
A rag, a mock at first—erelong,
When men have bled and women wept,
To guard its precious folds from wrong,
Even they who shrank, even they who slept,
Shall leap to bless it and to save,
Strike! For the brave revere the brave!

(Lebeson, Anita. *Recall to Life.* New York: Thomas Yoseloff, 1970.)

A Letter on Peoplehood (text, page 78)

Jacob Ossofsky, 18, was a corporal in the army during World War II. This letter to his parents, written during the war, shows that Jews from different backgrounds felt themselves part of one people.

Fort Bragg, N. C.
April 19, 1944

Dear Dad,
. . . Yesterday evening we had nothing to do and it was too dark outside for us to see any of the scenery as we sped by, so one of the fellows took out his harmonica and we began to sing. In my car there were quite a few Jewish boys and since the harmonica player was also a Jewish fellow, it was not long before we started to play and sing Jewish folk songs. We sang some songs that would have made you wonder how they ever came to young Jewish soldiers—"Lu Mir Alle In Einem Zein," "Mein Shtetele Beltz," "Mein Yiddishe Mama," "Der Rebbe Aleh Meilech," and so on. We also sang several Hebrew songs and the "Hatikvah." I sang many of the folk songs for them which I had learned from the Mittle Shule operettas. These songs were completely new to them.
It soon occurred to me that some of those fellows, who would probably never even have listened to a Jewish tune at home, now had, by means of these melodies (which held a different memory for each of them) sought and found a closely-knit feeling among themselves on this train.
It is interesting to note that among this group of boys there were a young Zionist, a German refugee, a boy from Chicago, several fellows from Brooklyn and Jersey, and others from all different sections of the country, and although we had never before seen one another, the rousing melody of the Jewish "schaer" brought us together as if we had been old-time pals.
Well, that's how we amused ourselves while riding along, forgetting, in the midst of our song, that we were getting farther away from home.
And now, I guess it's time to say goodbye. Don't worry.

Love,
Yankl

(Rontch, Isaac, ed. *Jewish Youth at War.* New York Marstin Press, *1945.)*

The Poetry of a Young Jew (text, page 103)

These two poems appeared in *The Flame*, the newspaper of the New York Union of Jewish Students. The poet is identified only as "Tagar." He (or she?) speaks about Jewish identity in America today.

FRIDAY NIGHT

friday nite
Shabbos
kiss the queen as she enters
blanketing her children in a tapestry of
holiness
semites from the upper west side
very high on homemade smoky rock religion

ten seconds of two thousand years
of tribal memories
little fleeting bits of eastern europe
together with new york ghetto
and so much fear of life and future

friday nite
and we all feel better
drinking israel's sweet wine
eating israel's magic herb
only flower in a garden of cement
only thing to take one away
from crowded smashed human togetherness

GHOSTS

where is izzy from the corner deli
and moish from the grocery
and al the butcher

they're here
right on
your block
now
with electric silly
gypsy suits
and fuzzy hair
and so much music

(Tagar (pseud.). *The Flame*. New York: City College, March, 1971.)

Community

Joining the Community (text, page 30)

In his study of Jews in suburbia, Albert Gordon quotes a characteristic feeling of Jews in America today. One of the main functions of a synagogue or temple is to unite Jews together as a community.

"Joining a temple brings me closer to people of my own faith and creates a common bond between me and them. Coming from a community which had a very small Jewish group, I can appreciate how important it is for Jews to have this kind of bond. [It does not matter whether] we feel that our learnings are Orthodox, Conservative or Reform. Even though we say that we are 'belonging because of our desire to give our children a Hebrew training', we are really benefiting ourselves because we are enriching our own lives through religious knowledge and our closeness to others of our faith." (Gordon, Albert. *Jews in Suburbia.)*

Jewish Self-Government (text, page 31)

In the mid-1700's, the Jews of Philadelphia drew up a synagogue constitution. We can see that one of the duties of the Jewish community leaders was to serve as judge.

Since we are concerned about the matter of creating an organized community, it is important that we exercise prudence in selecting communal leaders.

The members who select the Board of Five are hereby warned to be careful to choose people who will dispense justice.

. . . the Board of Five shall be careful, when they select a president, to see that he is neither quarrelsome nor tyrannical, but that he is a God-fearing man who is desirous of according justice to everyone.

Every householder is obligated to pay heed to what the president orders in the synagogue and, God forbid, not offer him any affront.

If there is a quarrel among the members, then the one in whom the quarrel centers must go to the president and to the Board of Five, and they must settle the matter. If however the litigant will not present himself, then the president has no right to give him a seat nor show him any religious courtesy in the synagogue, not to him, nor even to his children (as long as the children are subject to the litigant), until he submits to the president's decision. For the president is required to rent out the seats in order to support the synagogue. If, however, a person does not want to pay for his seat, then he has no right to a seat, nor to any congregational religious courtesy, not even to make a single donation in public.

If a person has insulted the synagogue and does not wish to submit, and the president decides that that man has done wrong, and that the affronter is to have no religious courtesy as long as he, the president, is in office, when, later on, another president comes to power, the new president is not to accord that man any religious courtesy until that offender has been examined by the new president and the Board of Five, to determine whether he was guilty or not. (Marcus, Jacob, ed. *American Jewry: Documents, Eighteenth Century.* Cincinnati: American Jewish Archives, Hebrew Union College, 1959.)

The Synagogue as Center of Jewish Life (text, page 44)

Here is an example of the sort of bulletin published by hundreds of Jewish congregations across the country today. As this newsletter shows, Shabbat, education, youth activities, social events, community welfare action, all of these take place at the local synagogue.

The Shofar

Synagogue service schedule
Friday Evening Service .... 8:00 P.M.
    Followed by Oneg Shabbat
Shabbat Morning Service .... 9:30 A.M.
Religious School to resume again in early September.

Yahrzeits
Benjamin Krupnick 28 Tammuz   July 10
Ann Cherry   9 Av   July 20

Shabbat candle lighting time
July 7 .... 7:45 P.M.
July 14 .... 7:40 P.M.
July 21 .... 7:37 P.M.
July 28 .... 7:32 P.M.

Onegs
July 7   Mr. & Mrs. George Flashner
in honor of the Bar Mitzvah of their son, Perry
July 14   Mr. & Mrs. Perry Schlein
July 21   Mr. & Mrs. Eric Goldby
in honor of Eric's birthday
July 28   Mr. & Mrs. Norman Cohen
in honor of the Bar Mitzvah of their son, Stuart

Speakers
July 7   Rabbi Art Blecher
July 14   Mr. Perry Schlein
July 21   Mr. Eric Goldby
July 28   Rabbi Leon Kagan

Mark your calendar now!
Reserve Saturday, August 5 for Etz Chayim Sisterhood's 1972 Summer Social.

Library glimpse
Library books are due now. No fine will be imposed if you return the books now! No questions asked.

Israel Interest Group
Israel Interest Group will have its first meeting, Sunday, July 9, 7:30 P.M. at the home of Mr. & Mrs. Yehuda beYaacov, Harrisburg Drive, S.E., Shmuel HarEl will speak about engineering in Israel. All are welcome! Please advise the host in advance so enough chairs will be set up to handle the crowd.

Our 1972 high school graduates
Lisa Barov, Suzanne Boyar, Bernie Flank, Sheree Greenbaum, Alan Herbin, Kathy Krupnick.

Bazaar news
"Dem bones, dem bones, Dem soup bones"! We need "soup bones" (circular, ½ inch thick, approximately) in very clean condition. Also, need leftover latex wall paint or other paints, brushes, lumber scraps. Could also use more interested ladies to help at the workshops. If you haven't been coming: Try it; You'll Like It. (*The Shofar*, Huntsville: Etz Chaim Cong.—Huntsville Cons. Syn., 1972.)

The German Jews' Reaction to the "Polacks" (text, page 76)

The Jews from Germany had been long established in American life by the time of the Eastern European wave of immigration. Rabbi Joshua Trachtenberg recalled how the "high-brow" German

Jews of his community in Pennsylvania first reacted to the "peasants" who poured in from Eastern Europe. This division has long since disappeared, and the two congregations are now thinking of merging.

The same forces that had driven Jews from Bavaria and other parts of Central Europe half a century before introduced to Easton a new contingent of migrants from Eastern Europe toward the end of the eighties. There was no common denominator between the two groups. In this short space of time the migrants from Germany had graduated from the rank of peddler to that of "businessman" (petty though the business might still be), had acquired enough status as Americans (in their own eyes, at any rate) to be disdainful of the "Polacks," and had moved so far away from the earlier religious pattern as to feel no kinship with those who were now repeating their own experience. One of the surviving members of that generation of German Jews admitted to me that, although he knew . . . [the immigrants] were entering the country in increasing numbers, he was not conscious of their presence virtually as his neighbors in the little city of Easton. Until recently there were still quite a number of older unmarried German-Jewish women who had been of marriageable age at the turn of the century; in the absence of eligible bachelors of their own group it simply never occurred to them and their parents that they might find mates among the young men from Eastern Europe.

The "Polacks," for their part, were contemptuous of the "Dietschen," with their "goyish" ways and their airs. In 1889 they founded their own Congregation, Bnai Abraham, strikingly reminiscent of the original Brith Sholom [German Reform Congregation] with the same ritual and mutual aid features. The two groups went their separate ways, with no points of contact; there were now two "communities," the older dying for want of fresh blood, the younger exuberant and rambunctious as the former had once been. The two synagogues were only one block apart. On the second day of Rosh Hashanah, one year, a "Polack" on his way to *shul*, passing the deserted Reform temple of the "Deitschen," hung a sign on the door: "Closed on account of holiday."(Trachtenberg, Joshua. *Publication of the American Jewish Historical Society*, Vol. XIII, 1952-1953.)

Family

The Land of Opportunity (text, page 23)

In his *Memoirs of a Practical Dreamer*, Benjamin Laikin describes his decision to leave his parents and go to America. America meant freedom for this young Jew, but it also meant breaking up the family.

One Saturday night we sat around the table chatting, my family and I. I contrasted for them the grim picture of a young Jew in a small town in Russia with the glowing possibilities of life for that same young man in free America, a land where truly a Jew could become President.

Perhaps it was that final argument, perhaps they were convinced all along but were reluctant to part with their son. In any event, it was on that night that my parents finally and reluctantly agreed.

"Perhaps you are right, my son," said my mother. "Go to America."

The very next day I made my way to Bobruisk where I contacted the man who would help me get across the border and on my way to America. I knew that the Police Commissioner would never give me the documents I would need for a government passport. A week later, on Sunday, just before Purim, I began my long-dreamed of, long-awaited journey to the United States.

Father took me to the train. I will never forget that scene. Father ran after the train as it began to roll down the tracks trying to keep abreast of the car in which I sat, my face glued to the window. I could see him biting his lips, tears welled up in his eyes. My own vision was blurred by the tears that filled mine. It was a moment that wrenched my heart. (Laikin, Benjamin. *Memoirs of a Practical Dreamer*. New York: Bloch Pub., 1971.)

Family Unity in Suburbia (text, page 53)

One of the things Albert Gordon reports about in *Jews in Suburbia* is family life. His survey shows that the Jewish emphasis on family unity remains strong among today's parents. How do you feel? Do you think family unity will continue to be strong among Jews, or will it decline in the future?

[The poll revealed that] Jewish families like to assemble on religious festivals and holy days in order to enjoy the occasion as a family unit. Indeed, the Passover Seder traditionally enjoined upon the Jew *must* center around the family table, where the story of the Exodus from Egypt is recounted and the implications of the ideal of human freedom are discussed. Father, mother and children join with other members of the family, not only to relive the experiences of that far-off day, but to enjoy the repast that follows the reading of the Passover narrative. The Jewish New Year, the Day of Atonement and other religiously significant days on the Hebrew calendar are directly associated with the family: family gatherings help the Jew to identify himself with traditional religious values.

Parents and children, grandparents, uncles, aunts and cousins—indeed, all those who comprise the extended family—frequently assemble on the Sabbath Eve and other joyful occasions because they "like to be together." Young married couples often speak with satisfaction of visiting their parents' home with their young children—especially on Sabbaths and festivals, when children may note the rich symbolism and ceremonial associated with these occasions. Grandparents speak of their delight when grandchildren who attend Hebrew or Sunday school classes are able to join in reciting the Hebrew prayers and to observe the ritual of the day . . .

[Our survey of suburban Jews showed] a startling uniformity in *all* the responses: however difficult it may be to travel longer distances, they are seldom absent from the parents' homes on the traditional Festival and Holy Days. As long as this Jewish emphasis upon the family continues, I believe, Jews in suburbia will manifest the same positive values that have characterized them in the past. (Gordon, Albert. *Jews in Suburbia.*)

The Language Gap *(text, page 66)*

The Yiddish language has not been transmitted to the younger generations of Jews. Some parents spoke Yiddish only when they didn't want their children to know what they were saying. This statement shows what happens to family unity when one generation speaks only Yiddish and another generation speaks only English.

"I sometimes wish that my children could really understand my parents. My folks are quite old-fashioned. They live over in Dorchester. They speak Yiddish mostly and only a little English. They talk to the children in English. The children like them, I know, but I'm sure that they don't really understand them. They don't know what they went through, how hard they worked to give my sisters, my brother and me a chance to get ahead. But I guess there's always a division between generations, and maybe we have no right to expect it to be different. Maybe that's why I try to see to it that we are all one happy family here in my home." (Gordon, Albert. *Jews in Suburbia.*)

Bintel Brief *Solves a Family Problem (text, page 68)*

In this letter to the advice column of the *Jewish Daily Forwards*, a Yiddish newspaper, we see a conflict between religious parents and non-observant children. Even though the *Forwards* itself usually took a non-religious position on issues, here the editors affirm the traditional Jewish emphasis on family unity.

1906

Dear Editor,

I am a Russian revolutionist and a freethinker. Here in America I became acquainted with a girl who is also a freethinker. We decided to marry, but the problem is that she has Orthodox parents, and for their sake we must have a religious ceremony. If we refuse the ceremony we will be cut off from them forever. Her parents also want me to go to the synagogue with them before the wedding, and I don't know what to do. Therefore I ask you to advise me how to act.

Respectfully,
J.B.

ANSWER:

The advice is that there are times when it pays to give in to old parents and not grieve them. It depends on the circumstances. When one can get along with kindness it is better not to break off relations with the parents.

(Golden, Harry, and Metzker, Isaac, eds. *A Bintel Brief*. New York: Doubleday & Co., 1971.)

Religion

The Evolution of Reform Judaism in America (text, page 47)

A study of The Reform Movement in America by David Philipson outlines typical patterns of development for Reform congregations. No two congregations followed the exact same pattern. From the two examples below, we can see that the first Reform congregations started out as traditional and reformed over a period of years.

CONGREGATION MICKVE ISRAEL
SAVANNAH, GA.

1. System of fines and penalties for violation of the Sabbath eliminated (1848).

2. Prayer for the government to be read in English (1854).

3. Men and women permitted to sit together during the rabbi's discourse (1857). By 1875, men and women are sitting together throughout the entire service. However, there is no mention when the latter reform was first instituted.

4. The following reforms were adopted February 11th, 1868:
   a) Elimination of second-day holiday.
   b) Introduction of mixed choir and organ.
   c) Abbreviated prayer ritual.
   d) Elimination of the *haftarah* (lesson from the prophets).

5. Marriage canopy (*huppah*) made optional, 1879-1880.

6. Hats made optional 1892-1894.

7. Union prayer book adopted, 1901.

8. Late Friday evening service instituted, 1904.

KAHL MONTGOMERY
MONTGOMERY, ALA.

1. System of fines and penalties for violation of holidays eliminated, 1861.

2. Mixed choir (men and women) introduced between 1862 and 1867.

3. Only one chapter read from the Torah *parashah* (weekly Pentateuchal portion). *Bar Mitzvah* boys, however, permitted to read entire *parashah*, 1822.

4. Organ introduced by 1873.

5. Temple Emanuel prayer book adopted, 1874.

6. Hats made optional, 1875-1883.

7. Confirmation (for boys and girls) instituted by 1880.

8. Late Friday evening service instituted by 1881.

(Philipson, David. *The Reform Movement in America.* New York: Ktav, 1967.)

Reaction against Sunday Services (text, page 47)

Here is a statement of the early Reform position concerning weekly services:

Whereas, we recognize the importance of maintaining the historical Sabbath as a bond with our great past and a symbol of the unity of Israel the world over; and,

Whereas, on the other hand, it cannot be denied that there is a very large number of Jews who, owing to economic and industrial conditions, are not able to attend services on our sacred day of rest; be it

Resolved, that in the judgment of this conference there is nothing in the spirit of Judaism to prevent the holding of divine service on Sunday or any other week day where the necessity for such service is felt. (Central Conference of American Rabbis. *Year Book.* Vol. XIV. 1904.)

Sabato Morais, a founder of Conservative Movement, criticized this Reform attitude.

I do not underestimate the fearful difficulties which stand in the way of Sabbath-keeping, and to my sorrow I have nothing new to propose to bring about its observance. I cannot join those in the clergy who offer inadmissible compromises and less can I agree with such as plan out schemes which will prove murderous stabs in the heart of historical Judaism. For in Sunday services I hear dirges sung over the death of my father's religion. (Davis, Moshe. *The Emergence of Conservative Judaism.* Philadelphia: Jewish Publication Society, 1963.)

The Reform Movement later moved away from the idea of holding major weekly congregational services on Sunday.

The Founding of the Jewish Theological Seminary of America (text, page 47)

The preamble to the constitution of the Jewish Theological Seminary Association, formed in 1885, shows that the Conservative Movement began as a reaction to the Reform Movement in America.

The necessity has been made manifest for associated and organized effort on the part of the Jews of America faithful to Mosaic Law and ancestral traditions, for the purpose of keeping alive the true Judaic spirit; in particular by the establishment of a seminary where the Bible shall be impartially taught and rabbinical literature faithfully expounded, and more especially where youths, desirous of entering the ministry, may be thoroughly grounded in Jewish knowledge and inspired by the precept and example of their instructors with the love of the Hebrew language and a spirit of devotion and fidelity to the Jewish Law. *(Students' Annual.* Jewish Theological Seminary, 1914.)

The Joys of Jewish Home Life (text. page 53)

A study of the Jewish community in America, published by the American Jewish Committee 1969, shows that most Jews have very positive childhood recollections of a warm, religious home life. Some people are able and willing to recreate that same joy in their own homes today. "Lakeville" is a fictitious name.

A young Lakeville lawyer (the son of an immigrant who owned a corner grocery) had discarded most of the dietary laws but practiced many other rituals. He recalled: "It was pleasant when we came home from school on Friday and celebrated Shabbes; we lit the candles and had real meals. We ate at all hours during the week."

An observant middle-aged clothing store owner reminisced about "Friday afternoon and the smell of Shabbes in the house— the fresh baked *challah,* the *gefilte fish.*"

A moderately observant Lakeville mother of two children remembered: "The excitement of the holidays! We always had lots of people for the Seder and on Sukkos. I used to enjoy the singing and the gaiety." Another informant remembered getting a new suit of clothes for Passover.

The Seder was recalled most frequently and, it seems, with the greatest warmth and sentiment—an embrace of ceremonial and familial memories. A manufacturer reminisced: "The rituals of Passover were most pleasant. All my relatives would be there, including fourteen children . . . My oldest uncle would say kiddish." (Sklare, Greenblum, Ringer. *Not Quite at Home.* New York: American Jewish Committee, 1969.)

Jewish Values in Suburbia (text, page 55)

A survey of modern suburban Jews posed this question: "Irrespective of whether you follow religious procedures or attend synagogue, do you consider yourself a religious person?" The answers showed that most Jews, whether ritually observant or not, share characteristically Jewish concepts: kindness, charity, honesty.

Some 15 per cent considered themselves "very religious," another 15 per cent "not at all religious," and the majority, 70 per cent, felt they were "somewhat" or "moderately" religious. The "very religious" most frequently conceived of religion in terms of moralism; they were generally satisfied with their own moral behavior, and did not feel themselves wanting in other religious dimensions. On the other hand, those who considered themselves "moderately religious" tended to see religion in terms of rituals.

The moralistic note was sounded by a man, brought up in a traditionally religious home, who felt that rituals mattered little. "They disappear," he said, "but not the innate very personal belief in God . . . I wouldn't hurt anyone, can't turn anyone down, and no one will walk out of my house hungry . . . My belief in religion is not in the hereafter, but rather in the hell and heaven here on earth and now. I don't believe in putting money into a church or *shul* as a premium on an insurance policy for the hereafter. I don't even have to go to *shul.*" Another respondent considers himself "very religious" because of his conduct, his honesty, his charity.

A woman, also of moralistic bent, said her concept of being a good Jew was "being a good person. I wouldn't do anything to hurt anyone. Just being religious [i.e., observant] doesn't make one a good person. Showing a non-Jew what a good person a Jew can be without ceremonials is what I believe. I have a belief in the Ten Command- ments . . . and I live it." To her, as to some other unobservant Jews, belief in God has become irrelevant in connection with being "very religious." In their view, God has been altogether supplanted by ethics, and the ethical performance is the real measure of religious value. (Sklare, *et. al. Not Quite at Home.*)

The Significance of Passover Today (text, page 75)

Here is a statement by a Jewish parent on the meaning Passover has for his family. He feels that the destruction of the six million Jews has given added importance to the Festival of Freedom.

Passover, commemorative of the Exodus from Egyptian bondage, is still a major festival in the Hebrew calendar. Indeed, Rabbis throughout suburbia note that the Passover Seder services in the home are more popular and even better attended than they were a decade ago, with approximately seventy-five to eighty per cent of Jewish families conducting or attending a Seder.

"Passover is so important to us because the Hebrew school and Sunday school spend so much of their time teaching our children how to observe the ritual of this festival. All the blessings and traditional chants are taught. The many symbols, colorful and beautiful, are a source of pleasure to the children.

Matzoh is 'different.' It looks and tastes different . . . The Seder is a home gathering where parents, children and guests join to tell the story of the Exodus of the Jews from Egypt, point up the importance of human freedom and the meaning of slavery. What lesson can have greater meaning to Jews in these days who remember Hitler, who know the evils of Fascism and Communism? So Passover, the Spring Festival, with its important message and its rich symbolism assumes greater meaning for Jews today. I notice that people prepare their homes for Passover much more carefully than they did a decade ago. Our children demand it of us . . ." (Gordon, Albert. *Jews in Suburbia.*)

Tsedakah

An Appeal to Aaron Lopez for Help (text, page 16)

Aaron Lopez was well-known throughout colonial America for his charity to both Jews and Gentiles. This letter from a poor woman in New York shows that the Jew can always be called upon to practice tsedakah.

Newyork, July 26, 1770.

Dear Sir:

I take the liberty once moor of troubling you in the letter way, which I hope you'l pardon. Necesseaity drives me to it. I am now in years and unable to do anny thing for my self. It's comeing to quarter [rent] day, and I am affraid I shall be troubled. I am helpt by my friends, but it is not sufficent to keep me from disstress. So, dear sir, I hope your heart, which is naturly tender, will be moved with kind compassion for a poor fellow creature who is labouring under greater distress than it's possible to express. What ever you do for me, I hope God will doubly return.

So, remain with great respect,

Your obedient servant,
Hannah Paysaddon

(Marcus, Jacob, ed. *American Jewry*.)

A Congregation Takes Care of the Community (text, page 33)

Dr. Joshua Trachtenberg was a rabbi in Easton, Pennsylvania, for many years. In his history of the Jewish community there, *Consider the Years*, Rabbi Trachtenberg describes how the Jews organized themselves to provide for the various needs of their fellow Jews. We can see that they considered tsedakah an everyday duty, rather than an occasional act of generosity.

In traditional fashion, [the congregation] dispensed charity widely as needed, in co-operation with the Ladies' Aid Society, and provided for the needs of transients and *meshulachim* (itinerant collectors for charitable institutions), putting them up in private homes until, in 1922, it acquired a house next door to the synagogue which became the *Hachnosas Orchim* (House of Shelter). The cemetery on the South Side was wholly owned and controlled by the congregation, which sold plots there to its members. The traditional *Chevra Kadisha* (Burial Society) gave their services at deaths and burials without compensation, and so zealously did they perform their self-appointed *mitzvah* that it was easy to believe they liked nothing better than a funeral. Early in the days of the automobile a member of the congregation was killed in an accident some distance from town. Four members of the *Chevra Kadisha* thereupon dutifully set out in a touring car to bring his body home. But the car was crowded, and the dead must be treated with proper respect. So they returned with the corpse seated upright in the back between two of them, solicitously resting its head alternately on their shoulders. (Trachtenberg, Joshua. *Consider the Years*. Easton: 1944)

Tsedakah in Providing for the Needy (text, page 44)

Here are two examples of congregations taking care of the sick, the aged, and the poor. The first letter is from an ailing widow to the Jewish congregation in New York City. She was being supported by the congregation, and here she asks for her usual grant.

In the second letter, the same congregation (the Spanish-Portugese, Shearith Israel) gives instructions for hiring a schoolmaster. Notice that children of poor parents are to be taught for free.

New Brunswik, 9 November, 1761.

Sir:

I take the liberty to wright to yow now. I think the at [that] is time for yow to get my wenters [winter's] . . . provisions, likewise a little money to bay some wood for the wenter. I woud a come down my self to feetchet [fetch it], but ben desebled, my legs heving swelds [swellings]. But y [I] hope, sir, that at ensent [that ancient proverb] not aut a sigt aut of mind [will apply to me].

Sir, hier y [I] lay sufering for the vant of wood and provisions. Y [I] remende, sir,

Your most humble servent,
Hanne Lezade

Remember my love to your espowse . . . and the reste of your familly.
(Marcus, Jacob, ed. *American Jewry*.)

New York, Dec. 16, 1760
Mr. Benj. Pereira

Sir:

. . . you will be good enough to engage . . . a suitable master capable to teach our children the Hebrew language. English and Spanish he ought to know, but he will not suit us unless he understands Hebrew and English at least . . . A single modest sober person . . . will be most agreeable. He must oblige himself to keep a publick school at the usual hours of the forenoons on every customary day at our jesiba. Children whose parents are in needy circumstances he must teach gratis. His salary ' shall be first at forty pounds, New York money per year, and shall commence from the day of his arrival here, and all other children he teaches must and will pay him as has been done heretofore. (*Publication of the American Jewish Historical Society*, Vol. XXVII, 1920.)

Immigrant Aid Societies (text, page 59)

Jews in America felt it was their duty to help the thousands of immigrants settle in the United States. Rather than leave tsedakah to chance, they formed organizations to accomplish their aims. The Jewish Protective Emigrant Aid Society issued this circular in 1886, outlining its objectives and methods.

1 . . . To assist immigrants on their arriving here to reach their respective place of destination, so that they may not all crowd in this city.

2 . . . To help them find their relatives and friends and communicate with them with a view to putting them under their protection and care.

3 . . . To obviate misunderstandings between the immigrants and the authorities at the busy Castle Garden reception center.

4 . . . To guard immigrants against impositions . . .

5 . . . To procure useful work and employment for the newcomers. (*American Jewish Archives*, Vol. III, No. 1, June, 1950.)

Justice

A Slave Returns to His Master (text, page 41)

This letter to Mordechai Sheftall tells an interesting story. Sheftall's slave had been stolen from him twenty years earlier, and now the slave wants to return to his old master. Jews in the South owned slaves, and Sheftall must have treated Tom better than Tom's Gentile masters.

Town of St. Mary's [Georgia],
5th October, 1796.

Mordecai Sheftall, Esq.,
Savannah.

Dear Sir:

About a week past, a negro man, who calls himself John, but says he was formerly named Tom, came to the garrison at Colerain [near St. Mary's] from St. Augustine. The account he gives is that he and his brother were taken from your cowpen near Briar Creek, during the [Revolutionary] War by the noted McGirt and carried to Florida and there sold; that he has had several masters, but the one from whom he run at this time is named McEnery, living in St. Augustine. He tells me that all his family belonged to you.

I brought him with me from Colerain, as the fellow was confined there. He is at my house, where, he says, he will remain until I hear from you, and to know whither [whether] you consider him as your property. I shall be glad to hear from you and to have a state of facts relating to this negro. With esteem, I remain,

Your humble servant,
James Seagrove

(Marcus, Jacob, ed. *American Jewry.*)

Inside the Sweatshop (text, page 61)

A labor union organizer by the name of Weinstein, together with three friends, visited several small factories in the 1890's. Here is Weinstein's description of what he saw. Notice that the workers themselves were afraid to complain!

It was Friday morning of a bleak fall day when Dr. Parkhurst [a famous Christian clergyman] came to our office accompanied by a friend of his, a medical doctor. I, together with A. Rosenthal, then delegate of the Kneepants Workers' Union, took them to investigate the men's tailor shops. We first stopped at No. 7 Ludlow Street, two houses from Canal. The delegate took us into a yard. Dirt was piled up to the windows. Scraps of goods and dirt were strewn over the narrow filthy stairs. The first shop we entered consisted of a small room with two little grimy windows and a still smaller chamber which had formerly served as a bedroom, without windows, only bars looking out on a dark hall. Several sewing machines stood in the first room. It was so small that we had difficulties in approaching the operators who sat very close to each other. Under the mantelpiece was the fireplace with a burning stove surrounded by flat-irons. The floors were filthy and littered with scraps of material. Several girls were sitting on the floor and working. They were the finishers.

Our appearance frightened the workers. They thought we were factory inspectors who had come to close the shop and throw them out of work. Dr. Parkhurst and his friend stood and shook their heads. We went over to the small dark chamber where the pressers worked, but could not enter because there was no room for us. A few bearded men stood there pressing the kneepants, bathed in sweat. The room being totally dark, they worked by the light of kerosene lamps. Suddenly the clergyman asked one of the pressers in German:

"How many hours do you work a day?"

"Eight hours," the old presser hastened to reply, fearfully. But the second presser mumbled: "We work eight hours on each side . . ."

He wanted to let us know that on both sides they worked sixteen hours a day. However, he was afraid to tell the truth in the presence of the boss.

On each floor of this tenement there were two shops where children's jackets, shirts and pants were made. In one of them, also a dark room, we found a shoemaker working at his bench. He had rented the space from the clothing contractor.

We encountered a synagogue in a sweatshop. Six days a week it was a shop; Friday evening and Saturday it became a house of worship. On entering this shop and seeing the *Oren-Kodish* [Holy Ark] near the sewing machines, the clergyman solemnly took off his high silk hat.

We made our way from one hell to another . . . The clergyman and the doctor were horribly depressed by all these scenes. (Epstein, Melech. *Jewish Labor in the U.S.* New York: Ktav, 1969.)

The Forwards *Leads the Fight for Justice (text, page 62)*

The Yiddish press helped rally the workers to organize themselves into unions and fight for their rights. The *Forwards* constantly printed reports of intolerable working conditions. Their advice was always: organize!

This letter is from the *Bintel Brief.* "Bintel Brief," or "bundle of mail," was the advice-to-the-reader column of the *Forwards.*

1908

Esteemed Editor,

We were sitting in the shop and working when the boss came over to one of us and said, "You ruined the work: you'll have to pay for it." The worker answered that it wasn't his fault, that he had given out the work in perfect condition. "You're trying to tell me!" The boss got mad and began to shout. "I pay your wages and you answer back, you dog! I should have thrown you out of my shop long ago."

The worker trembled, his face got whiter. When the boss noticed how his face paled, he gestured, spat and walked away. The worker said no more. Tired, and overcome with shame, he turned back to his work and later exclaimed, "For six years I've been working here like a slave, and he tells me,

'You dog, I'll throw you out!' I wanted to pick up an iron and smash his head in, but I saw before me my wife and five children who want to eat!"

Obviously, the offended man felt he had done wrong in not standing up for his honor as a worker and human being. In the shop, the machines hummed, the irons thumped, and we could see the tears running down his cheeks.

Did this unfortunate man act correctly in remaining silent under the insults of the boss? Is the fact that he has a wife and children the reason for his slavery and refusal to defend himself? I hope you will answer my questions in the "Bintel Brief."

Respectfully,
A.P.

ANSWER:

The worker cannot help himself alone. There is no limit to what must be done for a piece of bread. One must bite his lips till they bleed, and keep silent when he is alone.

But he must not remain alone. He must not remain silent. He must unite with his fellow workers and fight. To defend their honor as men, the workers must be well organized. (Golden, Harry, and Metzker, Isaac, eds. *A Bintel Brief.*)

A Sweatshop Owner Hears the Cry for Justice (text, page 62)

The *Jewish Daily Forwards* was read by Jews of all walks of life. The fact that this factory owner had a change of heart, shows that the Yiddish press had considerable impact upon its readers.

. . . We have a huge factory with our names on a big sign on the front of the building. But the bands that gave us our start are no longer made by us alone. We have many workers but have paid little attention to them since we were so involved with making our fortune.

In time I began to read your newspaper and, out of curiosity, even the "Bintel Brief," to see what was going on in the world. As I read more and more about the troubles, my conscience awoke and I began to think: "Robber, cold-blooded robber." My conscience spoke to me: "Just look at your workers, see how pale and thin and beaten they look, and see how healthy and ruddy your face and hands are."

This conscience of mine has a strong voice. It yells at me just as I yell at my workers, and scolds me for all my offenses against them. It will be enough for me to give just a few samples of my evil deeds: The clock in our shop gets "fixed" twice a day; the hands are moved back and forth. The foreman has on his table a stick like a conductor's baton and when someone says a word during working hours he hears the tick-tock of that stick. Our wages are never under two dollars or over seven dollars a week.

My conscience bothers me and I would like to correct my mistakes, so that I will not have to be ashamed of myself in the future. But do not forget that my brothers do not feel as I do, and if I were to speak to them about all this they would consider me crazy. So what is left for me to do? I beg you, worthy Editor, give me a suggestion.

Yours sincerely,
B.

ANSWER:
We are proud and happy that through the *Forward* and the "Bintel Brief" the conscience of this letter writer was aroused. We can only say to the writer that he must not muffle the voice of his conscience. He will lose nothing, but will gain more and more true happiness.
(Golden, Harry, and Metzker, Isaac, eds. *A Bintel Brief.*)

A Girl Leads a Strike for Justice (text, page 63)

The only way trade unions were able to achieve better wages and conditions, in the early days, was to strike. But the workers were usually afraid to take such a bold step. These newspaper articles show how one person was able to unite thousands of people into action.

The arrest on the picket line of two prominent women, Margaret Johnson and Mary Dreier, the latter, president of the newly organized New York Women's Trade Union League, attracted public attention to the situation in that trade. The reports in the *Forward* and in the English papers increased the excitement in the shops. About 2000 workers joined Local 25 during the first part of November. The general strike was on everybody's lips.

Heartened by the warm response, the committee of the local called a mass meeting in Cooper Union for November 22, 1909. The speakers included many prominent leaders: Gompers, Mary Dreier, Meyer London, Jacob Panken, J. Goldstein, B. Weinstein, Max Pine and B. Feigenbaum, chairman.

Cooper Union was jammed and thousands of men and women had to be directed to other halls. "For two hours," wrote an eyewitness, "the attentive audience (in Cooper Union) was cautioned to use due deliberation, to be sober in their decision, but to be loyal to each other and when they did decide to strike, to stand by their union until all demands were granted." Suddenly, Clara Lemlich, a young active striker of Leiserson and a member of the executive board of the local, arose and asked for the floor. There was instant commotion on the platform. Clara, "a wisp of a girl and still in her teens,"

was known in the trade and there was fear that her impulsiveness might upset the orderly course of the meeting. But Chairman Feigenbaum, scrupulously democratic, felt compelled to recognize her. Once on the platform, Clara Lemlich did not mince words. Impatiently she cried out in Yiddish:

"I am a working girl, one of those who are on strike. I am tired of listening to speakers who talk in general terms. What we are here for is to decide whether we shall or shall not strike. I offer a resolution that a general strike be declared *now*."

This simple and straight-forward motion swept the hall.

Instantly the big gathering was on its feet, everyone shouting an emphatic affirmative, waving hats, canes, handkerchiefs, anything that came handy. For five minutes perhaps, the tumult continued; then the chairman, B. Feigenbaum, made himself heard and asked for a seconder of the resolution. Again the big audience leaped to its feet, everyone seconding.

Carried off his feet by the emotional outburst, the chairman cried: "Do you mean it in absolute faith? Will you take the old Jewish oath?" And up came 2,000 hands with the prayer: "If I turn traitor to the cause I now pledge, may this hand wither from the arm I now raise!" (Epstein, Melech. *Jewish Labor in the U.S.)*

Social Action in the Reform Movement (text, page 105)

One of the main characteristics of the Reform Movement in America has been its concern for social action in the general community. This passage is taken from an article printed in the *Journal* of the Central Conference of American Rabbis. Its author, Reform Rabbi Henry Cohen, reminds his fellow rabbis that Jews have a religious duty to help all people, Jew and Gentile alike.

I am convinced that effective action [to help blacks] in the urban area is possible. However, such action would require a level of energy, expertise and expenditures towards which the organized Jewish community, and

particularly its religious institutions, are not even reaching.

Urgently needed in each major urban area is a staff of community-action oriented specialists (rabbinic and lay). Their roles would be: 1) To develop functional programs to meet desperate needs in housing, education, employment, etc. by drawing on the human and material resources of willing congregations and working with grass-root community groups on an equality of power basis to develop programs of mutual interest . . .

2) To develop advocacy techniques of using political power to pursue such crucial goals as low-cost mass transit, low-cost housing in the suburbs, higher minimum wage and the creation of jobs in the public sector when private industry has no use for millions of unemployed.

In these areas of conflicting interest, we rabbis should have something to say. As in any matter of distributive justice, we should not opt for Jewish interests out of pride or for black interest out of guilt. Rather should we weigh the consequences (short and long-term) of the various proposals and arrive at decisions based upon a deep probing of our moral commitments. The goal should be: a just accommodation between the various racial and ethnic groups in our cities. (Cohen, Henry. *Journal of the Central Conference of American Rabbis*, Vol. XIX, 1972.)

Education

Memories of Hebrew School (text, page 46)

Emily Seasongood wrote a description of her childhood in Cincinnatti in the 1860's. In this passage we see that complaints about having to learn Hebrew are over a century old.

A schoolhouse was in the annex of the synagogue which most all of the children of the members of the congregation attended. We were taught English and Hebrew. The *Chumish* I could not understand, and told my beloved father I could not see why it was taught us [in Hebrew] and please to have the teachers do away with it. As he was president of the congregation then, he brought it before the board, who quite agreed with me, and I was very happy after it was removed from our studies. Our teachers in English were Mrs. Rau and Mr. Bryan. Dr. Dessauer and Mr. Buttenwieser taught us German and Hebrew. Dr. Dessauer had a small cabinet in the corner of his room in which he always placed the stumps of his cigars, when he entered the room, and which he always smoked the following day.

Mr. Buttenwieser was a very small man and wore eyeglasses. He always called the pupils by their last name first when calling the roll. My cousin Betty Fechheimer was quite mischievous and would make him repeat her name until he became tired. He then took his rattan in his hand and said: "For that, Fechheimer Betty, come out before the class and receive your punishment." So she went to where he stood, took hold of the rattan, and danced him around the room. As he was nearsighted, he did not know she was close to him, and this was much to the amusement of the class. (Marcus, Jacob, ed. *Memoirs of American Jews 1776-1865*. Philadelphia: Jewish Publication Society, 1955.)

Modern Jewish Education (text, page 54)

Jewish educators today want students to enjoy their studies. Summer camps provide an opportunity for young people to learn about the Jewish way of life in a relaxed, pleasant atmosphere. In *A History of Jewish Education in the United States* Judah Pilch traces the development of Jewish educational camping.

Benderly's Camp Achvah (1926) first at Arverne, Long Island, then at Godeffroy, New York, had its impact on Jewish camping. Originally open only to Hebrew-speaking high school students, it later (1932) admitted non-Hebrew speaking Hebrew school seniors and even younger children. The camp preserved its Jewish educational goals by injecting Jewish themes into its art work—even into such activities as gardening. Formal Jewish studies were available to those interested in them. Sabbath and holiday programs were elaborate and impressive . . . Camp Achvah was an important experiment in both formal and informal Jewish educational camping . . . it stimulated the development of similar camps, among them Camp Massad [1943], Camp Yavneh [1944], Camp Sharon in Illinois, Camp Galil in Ohio [1944], Camp Ramah in Wisconsin [1946] . . . and several others.

. . . Camp Massad, as well as the Hebrew camp in general, sought to provide "a total and creative Hebrew and Jewish environ-

ment during the summer months of vacation."
It stressed the *Hebrew language* . . . religion
and observances . . . ethical concepts . . .
and Israel . . . the camp tried to give the
young child a positive attitude and com-
mitment to the existence and development
of the American Jewish community.

The Ramah camps—in Wisconsin, New
York, Pennsylvania, Massachusetts, California, and Canada—are operated by the United
Synagogue of America as a department of
the Teachers Institute of The Jewish Theological Seminary of America. They stress
Jewish religious observance (Conservative),
study, and the use of the Hebrew language,
in addition, of course, to the usual camping
activities. (Pilch, Judah. *A History of Jewish
Education in the United States.* New York:
American Association for Jewish Education,
1969.)

Education Conflicts with the Family (text, page 55)

Family loyalty and education are both primary Jewish values. This
letter to the Editor of the *Forwards* describes a situation in which
these two values conflicted. The paper's answer solves the dilemma
without sacrificing either value.

1907

Worthy Editor,

Allow me a little space in your newspaper
and, I beg you, give me some advice as to
what to do.

There are seven people in our family—
parents and five children. I am the oldest
child, a fourteen-year-old girl. We have been
in the country two years and my father, who
is a frail man, is the only one working to
support the whole family.

I go to school, where I do very well. But
since times are hard now and my father
earned only five dollars this week, I began
to talk about giving up my studies and going
to work in order to help my father as much
as possible. But my mother didn't even want
to hear of it. She wants me to continue my
education. She even went out and spent ten
dollars on winter clothes for me. But I didn't
enjoy the clothes, because I think I am doing
the wrong thing. Instead of bringing something into the house, my parents have to
spend money on me.

I have a lot of compassion for my parents.
My mother is now pregnant, but she still
has to take care of the three boarders we
have in the house. Mother and Father work
very hard and they want to keep me in school.

I am writing to you without their knowledge, and I beg you to tell me how to act.
Hoping you can advise me, I remain,

Your reader,
S.

ANSWER:

The advice to the girl is that she should obey
her parents and further her education, because in that way she will be able to give
them greater satisfaction than if she went
out to work.

(Golden, Harry, and Metzker, Isaac, eds.
A Bintel Brief.)

The Woman's Role in Jewish Life (text, page 55)

One of the functions of a value system is to tell the individual
where he or she fits into the overall society. Anita Lebeson, in *Recall to Life*, analyzes the inferior status women used to have in
traditional Jewish life.

It was the men who delivered the sermons, exhorted the multitudes, evolved the law and its interpretation, decreed the folkways and mores to implement daily life. They wrote the books, studied the stars, made the maps and the instruments for navigation, led the pilgrimages of escape. They wrote most of the letters, kept the chronicles, inventoried possessions, made the wills, listed business assets and losses. They governed and administered synagogues. They made long business journeys and petitioned governments and advanced moneys for exploration and sought lands of refuge and led many an exodus in search of sanctuary.

What of the women? The Jewish woman accepted the masculine decrees which governed her lot with an inner grace which betokened an inner strength. She adapted herself to the lesser role, the silent role in communal affairs, the accepting role in religious doctrine, the illiterate role in a world and a way of life in which literacy was the highest good. She toiled endlessly in market place and home to liberate her husband and her sons for a life of scholarship. Her place in the synagogue was symbolic. She sat in balconies behind lattice-worked grilles or curtained-off spaces, invisible, often unable to read a line in her prayer-book, depending on some woman reader who could both follow and translate the words on the holy page. Or if "educated" she could read a truncated version of the Bible especially prepared for her "small" mind, the "teitch-humesh" . . . (Lebeson, Anita. *Recall to Life.*)

The Forwards *Calls for Women's Emancipation (text, page 68)*

People wrote to the "Bintel Brief" column of the *Jewish Daily Forwards* for advice on all kinds of problems. Through their answers, the editors of the Yiddish press helped teach important new values to their readers.

1910

Dear Editor,

Since I do not want my conscience to bother me, I ask you to decide whether a married woman has the right to go to school two evenings a week. My husband thinks I have no right to do this.

I admit that I cannot be satisfied to be just a wife and mother. I am still young and I want to learn and enjoy life. My children and my house are not neglected, but I go to evening high school twice a week. My husband is not pleased and when I come home at night and ring the bell, he lets me stand outside a long time intentionally, and doesn't hurry to open the door.

Now he has announced a new decision. Because I send out the laundry to be done, it seems to him that I have too much time for myself, even enough to go to school. So from now on he will count out every penny for anything I have to buy for the house, so I will not be able to send out the laundry any more. And when I have to do the work myself, there won't be any time left for such "foolishness" as going to school. I told him that I'm willing to do my own washing but that I would still be able to find time for study.

When I am alone with my thoughts, I feel I may not be right. Perhaps I should not go to school. I want to say that my husband is an intelligent man and he wanted to marry a woman who was educated. The fact that he is intelligent makes me more annoyed with him. He is in favor of the emancipation of women, yet in real life he acts contrary to his beliefs.

Awaiting your opinion on this, I remain,

Your reader,
The Discontented Wife

ANSWER:

Since this man is intelligent and an adherent of the women's emancipation movement, he is scolded severely in the answer for wanting to keep his wife so enslaved. Also the opinion is expressed that the wife absolutely has the right to go to school two evenings a week. (Golden, Harry, and Metzker, Isaac, eds. *A Bintel Brief*.)

The Importance of Education (text, page 78)

Harry Golden reminisces about his childhood in the early 1900's in New York City.

I am willing to bet that between 1905 and 1914 there were more classrooms in operation in the fifteen square blocks of the Lower East Side than in some of the states of the Union. There were night schools, day schools, before-going-to-work schools, private schools, business schools, schools for learning English, and classes in "civics" (protocol for learning to be a citizen). There were schools located in tenement houses conducted by fellows who had come to America only a year before, and schools in settlement houses conducted by eighth-generation Christian social workers.

Education was the key to everything. You walked up to your flat in a tenement house and from behind every second door would come the shouting and the arguments over the issues of the day. Meanwhile the kids emptied out the local branch of the public library. "Have you started it yet?" That meant *Les Misérables* by Victor Hugo, a graduation of sorts. There was a rumor that it took six months to read. You went into training for *Les Miserables*.

Even the old folks were concerned with *education*. Your mother or your teacher dropped a bit of honey on the first book that was placed before you. You licked the honey to associate forever *sweetness* with *learning*. (Golden, Harry. *The Greatest Jewish City in the World*. New York: Doubleday & Co., 1972.)

A Jewish Publisher Meets the Needs of Young People (text, page 91)

A recent survey undertaken by the National Curriculum Research Institute (part of the American Association for Jewish Education) revealed some of the educational needs of Jewish students in America today:

In questioning some 810 teenagers and young adults in five communities, the NCRI discovered some of the major concerns of these young people. They are bothered about the relationships between Diaspora Jewry and Israel, the sociological status and definition of the Jewish people, attitudes toward other religious groups, the difficulty in acquiring adequate knowledge of Bible and Jewish literature and philosophy, and the place of Hebrew.

If you had been asked, what would you have given as your concerns?

A modern publisher of Jewish educational materials, Behrman House Inc., distributed a curriculum guide for Jewish schools. The following excerpt from that guide shows how the intellectual needs of the students are turned into "areas" of instruction.

AREAS OF INSTRUCTION

Faith and Practice—Bible: Torah; Prophets; Writings.
Ethics: Personal; Social.
Prayerbook: Comparative religion.
Introduction to Jewish belief.

Community—History: Medieval; Modern; American;
Survey. State of Israel.
American Jewish sociology.

Hebrew—Mastery of basic skills.
Simple Biblical texts. Siddur.

Schoolwide activities—Dance. Newspaper. Choir.
Dramatics. Tzedakah. Music. Worship.
Holiday celebrations. Assemblies.

(*A Behrman House Guide for the Jewish School*. New York: Behrman House Inc., 1972-1973.)

Integration

The First Jewish Prayer in Congress (text, page 26)

In 1860, Dr. Morris J. Raphall became the first rabbi to deliver the opening prayer of the House of Representatives. The event created a national stir, as can be seen from this report of a Jew who was present in the gallery.

. . . As the minute hand of the large clock opposite the Speaker's chair was approaching the hour of noon, a kind of impatient expectation seemed to prevail in the galleries which was interrupted by a buzzing sound, "There he is," and every eye was turned towards the Speaker's chair. Next to that chair, but one step lower, was seated an old man with a *Tallith* over his shoulders, and a velvet cap on his head. I at once recognized the Rev. Dr. Raphall, whose lectures on the Poetry of the Bible I had attended ten years ago, at Savannah. He appeared fatigued; and, as he looked languidly around him, I asked myself, How would I feel if, young and strong, and business-man as I am, I were about to address two hundred and fifty of the most talented and gifted men in the country, besides the immense crowds in the galleries, whose feelings [are not] prejudiced in my favor? and, as I did not feel quite sure of my own moral courage, I began to doubt whether that pale old man would have nerve enough for the occasion . . .

Many of the Congressmen thought it was in bad taste for Rabbi Raphall to wear a *tallit* and a *yarmulke* inside the chamber, but one Representative showed a deep understanding of the concept of religious equality.

. . . [T]he Rabbi did right in adhering to his costume; he came among us to pray according to his faith. For the moment, the Hall of Congress was his Synagogue. He had to maintain the perfect equality of his persuasion and of its religious practices, with that of any other denomination. [If he had] departed from the regular practice of the Synagogue, if he had yielded to our habits, so far as to come with his head uncovered, and without his vestments which a Jewish Rabbi wears at the time of solemn service, such concession to our views and feelings would also have been renouncing of that perfect equality which it was his duty as a Jew and a minister of religion to uphold . . . (Korn, Bertram W., *Eventful Years and Experiences*. Cincinnati: American Jewish Archives, 1954.)

The Sabbath Conflicts with Life in America (text, page 52)

Here is a memoir written by an immigrant from Eastern Europe in the early 1900's. The necessity of earning a living in the "land of opportunity" forced this man to violate one of his strongest beliefs.

The work was hard. The day was long and hot. Suddenly I realized that I was working on the Sabbath. I thought to myself, my father and the other Jews back home [in Europe] are in the Synagogue now. It was time for the reading of the weekly Torah portion. A deep sadness came over me. My heart was heavy with guilt and shame. Was it for this that I had come to America? To become a rag picker and desecrate the Sabbath? The agony loosed a flood of tears that I could not control. My Negro co-worker didn't understand what was happening but his sympathy was quick and genuine. He tried to console me. He patted my shoulder and spoke softly to me. Later he brought me a pitcher of beer and made me drink some of it. "It'll make you feel better," he said.

Before coming to America I had never seen a black man. When I did see my first colored person, I must confess I was surprised, and also a bit frightened. Somehow that act of friendship, of humanity, that drink of beer helped to break down the wall I myself had put between us.

The boss came over to us. He too spoke gently and calmed me down. Still, I could not shake off the feeling that I was facing a terrible battle for survival in this golden land. (Laikin, Benjamin. *Memoirs of a Practical Dreamer.*)

Processing of Immigrants at Ellis Island (text, page 58)

Here is a description of conditions on Ellis Island in the early 1900's. The medical examination was just part of the screening process immigrants had to undergo before being allowed to enter the United States. They had left Europe for the "land of opportunity," and this was their first experience when they arrived.

When [the immigrants] finally landed [at Ellis Island], the ground still seemed to sway under their feet as they dragged children and bundles along the walk toward the imposing red brick building. There was more shouting and pushing from guards who made them stand together in groups according to big numbers on the tags tied to their coats. An interpreter yelled out the numbers in German, Polish, Hungarian, Italian and Russian.

One by one, groups of thirty people at a time moved slowly forward, through the big door into dark tiled corridors, then—jostling two or three abreast—up a steep flight of stairs . . .

The immigrants at the top of the stairs were not given any more time to stand and stare. "This way! Hurry up!" an interpreter shouted in several languages, and they were pushed along one of the dozens of metal railings which divided the whole floor into a maze of open passageways. Although they did not realize it, they were already passing their first test as they hastened down the row in single file. Twenty-five feet away a doctor, in the smart blue uniform of the U.S. Public Health Service, was watching them carefully as they approached him. All children who looked over two years old were taken from their mothers' arms and made to walk.

It took only a few moments for the immigrants to reach the doctor, but that was time enough for his sharp eyes to notice one man who was breathing too heavily, a woman who was trying to hide her limp behind a big bundle, and a young girl whose shuffle and bewildered gaze might have been symptoms of a feeble mind. As each immigrant paused in front of him, the doctor looked hard at his face, hair, neck and hands; at the same time, with an interpreter at his side to help, he asked short questions about the immigrant's age or work to test his alertness. When a mother came up with children, each child in turn, starting with the oldest, was asked his name to make sure that he was not deaf or dumb.

In the doctor's hand was a piece of chalk; on the coats of about two out of every ten or eleven immigrants who passed him he scrawled a large white letter—"H" for possible heart trouble, "L" for lameness, a circled "X" for suspected mental defects, or "F" for a bad rash on the face. Then the immigrants filed on to a second doctor who was looking for diseases specifically mentioned in the law as reasons for deportation: signs of tuberculosis, leprosy, or a contagious skin disease of the scalp called *favus*. . .

At the end of the aisle interpreters waved immigrants whose coats were unmarked back toward the main part of the Registry Hall. But those whose coats bore chalk letters were pushed aside into a "pen," an area enclosed by a wire screen, to wait for more detailed medical examinations by other doctors. If they had any of the diseases proscribed by the immigration laws, or seemed too ill or feeble-minded to earn their living, they would be deported. One sobbing mother was pushed into the enclosure to wait with her little girl of eight or nine. The law said a parent had to accompany any very young child who was deported; but children of ten or older were sent back to Europe alone and simply released in the port from which they had sailed. Several weeping families in the hall were trying to make a terrible decision— "Shall we all go back together? Who will stay?" (Novotny, Ann. *Strangers at the Door*. Riverside: Chatham Press, Inc., 1971.)

Return to the Soil (text, page 60)

The Jewish farm movement, *Am Olam*, changed the Jew's view of himself and proved he could be a self-reliant citizen on American land. Joseph Brandes tells about the Jew's new self-image and the effect of that image on the Gentile community.

Unlike the Zionist groups, the Am Olam had no clear desire to work toward a Jewish state; their mother tongue was Yiddish, but they did not feel compelled to perpetuate it. Some undoubtedly preferred the Russian language and culture. They were torn between a consciousness of being Jewish and a sense of unity with the whole world. Nor did the socialistic aspects of Zionism appeal to many: among those who settled in the Carmel colony of New Jersey were a few of strong socialist convictions, but in a country where private enterprise was the secular faith they made little headway. Clearest of all was the belief that a return to the soil was the path to recognition and self-respect. "We chose the 'land of the brave and the home of the free'" said Sidney Bailey, one of the successful pioneer settlers, "and we came

here, instead of going to Palestine, which was then under a Turkish regime. . . . Our goal was to own a home and land as a means of earning a livelihood . . . to get the blessings of a natural life from heaven and earth . . . to become true citizens of our adopted country."

The *Vineland Evening Journal* gave favorable reports of such items as, "The Hebrews of the Woodbine Agricultural College have planted seven hundred fruit trees this fall." And the *Trenton Gazette* concluded in [April 29] 1904 that the "graduates of the Baron de Hirsch School have taught South Jersey a lesson . . . of adaptability to environment . . . a determination to make the best of conditions . . . the strength of overcoming racial prejudice." Where natives had failed to bring about development, "it was left to an alien people to perfect the growth in the wilderness." Both communities could work harmoniously toward a better future for Woodbine and Cape May County, for in

"the principle of give and take is [found] the true method of assimilation." (Brandes, Joseph. *Immigrants to Freedom*. Philadelphia: University of Pennsylvania Press, 1971.)

An Immigrant Americanizes Himself *(text, page 77)*

Dr. George M. Price was a Russian intellectual who emigrated to the United States in the 1880's. This excerpt from his diary shows that even the most intelligent man can be made to feel like a fool when he doesn't know the customs of a new environment.

I decided to look for work. To do this, however, I had to change my outer appearance, because my long hair, my pince-nez, the top coat and the Realschule [technical high school] uniform could hardly help me find employment. I, therefore, went to a nearby store and ordered American working clothes. The storekeeper, an exploiter, gave me yellow trousers and a shirt of the same color and a hat of an antediluvian style. All this cost five dollars, while the regular price for an American was no more than fifty cents. Then I went to the barbershop where for sixty-five cents—about a ruble and twenty-five kopecks—[the barber] clipped my hair to

the roots with some machine. I was finally a real American. But when I put on the so-called American attire and went out into the street, I was pursued by a crowd of youngsters and passers-by who stopped and laughed at me. I was again in trouble. At first I was a greenhorn, but why do they laugh at me now? I learned to my dismay that the swindler, the storekeeper, gave me clothes not worn by the workingmen, but by inmates of an asylum. I had to dump these clothes into the sea, preferring to appear as a greenhorn rather than as an insane person. (*Publication of the American Jewish Historical Society*, Vol. XLVII, 1957-1958.)

Disillusionment over the Land of Opportunity *(text, page 77)*

Adjustment to new life styles was very difficult for the immigrant, and this letter to "Bintel Brief" points out some common problems. The writer is worried that her son will not turn out right. Should her husband shave his beard?

1906

Worthy Editor,

We are a small family who recently came to the "Golden Land." My husband, my boy and I are together, and our daughter lives in another city.

I had opened a grocery store here, but soon lost all my money. In Europe we were

in business; we had people working for us and paid them well. In short, there we made a good living but here we are badly off.

My husband became a peddler. The "pleasure" of knocking on doors and ringing bells cannot be known by anyone but a peddler. If anybody does buy anything "on time," a lot of the money is lost, because there are some people who never intend to pay. In addition, my husband has trouble because he has a beard, and because of the beard he gets beaten up by the hoodlums.

Also we have problems with our boy, who throws money around. He works every day till late at night in a grocery for three dollars a week. I watch over him and give him the best because I'm sorry that he has to work so hard. But he costs me plenty and he borrows money from everybody. He has many friends and owes them all money. I get more and more worried as he takes here and borrows there. All my talking doesn't help. I am afraid to chase him away from home because he might get worse among strangers. I want to point out that he is well versed in Russian and Hebrew and he is not a child any more, but his behavior is not that of an intelligent adult.

I don't know what to do. My husband argues that he doesn't want to continue peddling. He doesn't want to shave off his beard, and it's not fitting for such a man to do so. The boy wants to go to his sister, but that's a twenty-five dollar fare. What can I do? I beg you for a suggestion.

Your constant reader,
F.L.

(Golden, Harry, and Metzker, Isaac, eds. *A Bintel Brief.*)

The Future of Jewishness (text, page 85)

Speaking about the role of the Jewish Community Center, Graenum Berger expresses his fears that Jews may become totally assimilated. Because the Jews are free to live as they choose in America, will we one day lose our identity as a people?

Jews are in danger of completely losing their straight-line rootedness to the God of Israel and may find themselves living only as alienated individuals in a society that expects them to convert as the price of acceptance.

Jews are in danger of losing their precious sense of history and may be condemned like most people to live only in the present.

Jews are in danger of losing their [uniqueness] and may be levelled to behave like everyone else.

Jews are in danger of being smugly satisfied to live in Galut [exile] permanently and may no longer bear the age old longing to return to Zion, the symbol of man's eternal struggle for a better world.

This impels me to press the Jewish Community Center . . . to assume the only function which can be deemed uniquely Jewish in this country—*to teach Jews how to live as Jews in the United States of America.* (Berger, Graenum. *The Jewish Community Center.* New York: Jewish Education Committee Press, 1966.)

Anti-Semitism

Resentment against Jews (text, page 29)

Here, Albert Gordon describes the vague anti-Semitic undertones
in a suburb of Boston. We can see a difference between the "official" views of the Gentile community and the private feelings of
some individuals.

In one of the elementary schools in a pre-
dominately Jewish section of Newton, an
"anti-kike" club of youngsters in the sixth
grade was discovered.

Due to the overcrowded condition of Newton High School, a new high school is now
under construction. It so happens that the
greatest growth of school population has
occurred in an area which is largely populated
by Jews. The high school will be built in
this district. Designed to house fifteen hundred
students, the new school will be of unusual
design and will provide facilities which no
school in Newton has ever had. One hears
people asking: "Isn't it strange that the Jews
should be getting the new high school, while
the rest of us get only what's left? We all
pay taxes, but the Jews get the best of us
all."

. . . Despite these undercurrents of tension and "feelings," the formal relations between the Jewish and non-Jewish communities in Newton is good. If [an occasional]
remark by a teacher in a classroom or a
policeman on his beat [is offensive to Jews]
Jewish families [usually see it] as an isolated,
[thoughtless] statement, rather than an in-
dication that a virulent anti-Semitism is
sweeping the suburb.

Invitations to speak at various Protestant
and Unitarian churches in Newton are frequently extended to the several Rabbis. Inter-
faith luncheons and "get-togethers" have
been sponsored by the women of the synagogues and churches in Newton for some
years with marked success. In 1957, the
women of the Sacred Heart Church (Catholic)
and their priest accepted the invitation of
Temple Emanuel's Sisterhood and thus became the first Catholic organization in Newton to visit their Jewish neighbors under
synagogual auspices. (Gordon, Albert. *Jews in
Suburbia.*)

The JDL Reacts to Persecution (text, page 35)

Ruth Buchbinder gives us an eye-witness report of a typical action
of the Jewish Defense League. The JDL believes that if Jews don't
learn to defend themselves by force, they will all be destroyed by
enemies.

It was 4:15 p.m., May 9, when the police
truck parked opposite Temple Emanu-El
on New York's Fifth Avenue. . . . Foot
policemen began to gather in groups of twos
and threes and stationed themselves in front
of the grand entrance of the temple whose
Sabbath services were to commence at 5:15.

A tall police captain was in the center
of about thirty men, and he was doing the
talking . . . I turned to [one] man and asked,
"Who are you and whom do you represent?"
He didn't reply, but from inside his jacket he
pulled out a heavy metal object that looked
to me like some kind of wrench. "If Forman

comes," he said—and brandished his weapon. He did not have to elaborate. James Forman is the black militant who had interrupted services at Riverside Church the previous Sunday to read his demands for church reparations to Negroes.

. . . the men divided themselves into two groups and lined up like soldiers, standing at attention, on either side of the entrance to the temple. Each held at his side a baseball bat. At least one, as I had seen, had a concealed metal weapon.

Many wore yarmulkes. Slowly their identification badges were placed on their lapels. They were stalwarts of the Jewish Defense League, under orders not to answer any questions.

I joined another group of men standing at the curb opposite the double rows of the armed JDL.

"'That's the most outrageous sight I ever saw," I remarked to anyone.

"It's about time the Jews stood up for themselves." one man replied.

"You approve of the vigilantes?"

"Listen, lady," he said, "I just came here from Germany. My parents were killed in a concentration camp. It started there just because of people like Forman."

"It started there," I answered above the rising tide of my blood pressure, "just because of hoodlums like those."

Another man joined in. "In Germany, nobody lifted a finger when the Nazis started. Not even Jews. We've finally learned. That's why they're here," pointing to the JDL.

"The police are here," I answered. "Nobody asked the JDL to come and protect Temple Emanu-El. Forman has every right to enter. Only the police can arrest him if he interrupts the worship service. Who needs them?"

"I don't give a damn about the Reform Jews inside," a second man said. "But I care about the temple because it's a symbol of Judaism."

"And those Jews carrying bats and metal objects—are they a symbol of Judaism?"

"Damn right," he said.

A young girl . . . was reduced to near hysteria by the same kind of comment. "That isn't Judaism!" she cried over and over again, as she pointed to the "bat-men" of the Jewish Defense League.

(Buchbinder, Ruth. *Congress Bi-Weekly.* Vol. 36, No. 8, May 26, 1969.)

A Jew Defends His Honor (text, page 41)

The following account has been pieced together from diaries in the possession of the American Jewish Archives of Hebrew Union College in Cincinnati. Dr. Philip Minis was a native-born Savannah Jew, and James Jones Stark a Gentile. Not only did Minis refuse to put up with Stark's jibes, but he responded in the manner of a proper Southern gentleman.

Aug. 9th, 1832

This difficulty took its origin from abuse uttered by Stark last spring at Luddington's barroom. Stark, when Minis was not present, one night, without any provocation, cursed Minis for a "damned Jew," a "damned Israelite," "he ought to be pissed upon," "he was not worth the powder and lead it would take to kill him," and abuse of a similar character. Some person had gone to Minis and told him that he was very much abused by Stark round at Luddington's, and he had better go there . . .

While the company were still at the bar, taking the drink to which they had been invited by him, on our difficulty being settled. Minis entered the room, and John informs me that on seeing [Minis] enter, [Stark] exclaimed: "Minis, I am damned glad that you have come here." Minis stayed a long time in company, but Stark said not one word about him. When Minis asked me what S. had said about him, I refused to tell him, observing that he, Stark, had had an opportunity of saying it that night before his face; and, as he had not done it, I thought that what he had said ought to be a matter of indifference.

Minis then wrote to Stark, saying that as he, S., had confessed doing an unnecessary injustice to him, M., he demanded an apology, or that satisfaction which one gentleman should afford another. This letter was written July.

August 9th at 12 m.

Stark sent Minis an answer that he should have satisfaction, and Mr. Wayne would make the necessary arrangement. Mr. Wayne [Stark's second] handed in his articles, to fight with rifles at five that afternoon. Spalding [Minis' second] objected to them. He objected to the rifle as unusual, but if his friend [Minis] could obtain satisfaction no other way, he accepted the rifle as the weapon, with certain provisos, which he submitted as articles to be agreed on between him and Wayne. The time fixed on was instantly rejected as being too soon, and before Spalding left, I observed that were I in Minis' place, I would not fight with so unusual a weapon, and such a short notice . . .

Minis' rifle was then at the gunsmith's [but] Wayne [Stark's second] said he must insist on his articles, and according to one of them, he and Stark would be together at Seriven's Ferry at five that afternoon. Spalding said verbally that it would be of no use, for that neither he nor his principal could possible be there. Wayne and Stark accordingly proceeded there, made a flourish, shot rifles, etc., and returned to town flushed with a victory

August 10th

. . . 10 P.M. This has been an eventful day. At a little past twelve Stark and Minis met at the City Hotel, when M. pronounced S. a coward. S. advanced and, Spalding says, put his hand in his pocket and drew something (he could not ascertain precisely what), when Minis drew and shot Stark through the upper part of the left part of the thorax. [The bullet] passed behind the top part of the scapula, and th[r]ough it into the side of the door which leads back from the barroom of the hotel. (*American Jewish Archives*, Vol. VII, No. 1, January 1955.)

Stealing across the Border (text, page 57)

The risks which this young man took to get to America show how hopeless life in Russia must have been for Jews.

I had been under the impression that stealing across the border would be child's play. My agent had taken my money and was supposed to supply me with everything I would need, including passage on the ship. He instructed me to go to Lublin, go to a certain hotel and give them a password. The hotel was an evil looking, ill-smelling inn. A man came to me and told me we would make the crossing that night. One look at the man was enough to freeze the blood in my body. He had the face of a highwayman and when he asked me to buy him a drink my fears multiplied.

We traveled by train all night. We dismounted at a small railroad station and there the man turned me over to a peasant with whom I had no means of communication. He was a Pole and did not speak Russian. I was stopped by a policeman who examined my resident's passport. He regarded me and the passport with suspicion and was on the verge of arresting me when a bribe allayed his doubts and I was again free. The peasant led me to a barn where I found some 70 men, women and children, both Jewish and non-Jewish. All were waiting to steal across the border.

Not one of them knew where we were or how far we were from the border. At night two other peasants appeared and motioned for us to follow them. We filed out of the barn, each carrying his bundle or basket, and made our way along the back roads.

Some of the women carried babies in their arms as well as packs on their backs. A few fell; their burdens were too heavy. They did not trust the men to carry their children, and their few meager belongings were also too valuable to trust to anyone else—even to a fellow Jew.

We walked most of the night, stopping at intervals to rest. In the morning we were divided into smaller groups and led to some stables where we let ourselves sink wearily to the ground. We were warned not to make a sound. Came the night and we continued our journey. By then we numbered some 300 souls. We had no idea where we were nor who the men were. We were completely at their mercy. It was dark and we had to keep moving. If anyone halted the peasant would prod him on with a stick.

The ground under our feet suddenly became softer. We were passing through a forest. Soon we were led into a swamp with the water reaching up to our knees. A Jewish woman with two children, a girl of about twelve and a child of three had be-come attached to me and clung to me as we made our way. The poor woman kept crying for fear that I would leave her stranded. I tied her child on my back. I held my basket in one hand and with the other hand held onto the woman. The girl held on to her mother's skirt.

The weather, bad to begin with, became worse. The rain combined with gusts of wind, slashed at our faces. Suddenly several shots rang out. The mother halted in the water, petrified. She gripped my hand in a clutch of iron. Some began to cry and the peasants ran among them hitting them with their sticks to quiet them.

After a while we were led off in another direction. We walked for about an hour and came to the edge of a lake. The peasants drove us into the water with their sticks. We waded in until the water reached up to our waists. And then, suddenly, we were on the other side. We had crossed the border! (Laikin, Benjamin. *Memoirs of a Practical Dreamer.*)

American Jews Protest the Pogroms (text, page 58)

In *Immigrants to Freedom,* Joseph Brandes describes the efforts of the American Jewish community on behalf of the Russian Jews in the 1800's. Even though the Jews were able to rally the support of the Gentile community, the most anyone could do in those days was help the refugee who escaped. How does this compare with our efforts to help Soviety Jewry today?

Throughout the era of persecution in Russia, the American conscience was never stilled. In Philadelphia, State Senator Horatio Gates Jones and Mayor King joined early in the relief plans proposed by the local chapter of the Alliance. . . . Speaking for "most of the Christian ministers," too, the Reverend R. H. Harper expressed his "horror at the treatment of the Jews" and desire to assist in the refugee relief campaign: Volunteers, including many non-Jews, provided medical care, food, and employment services to the thousands of refugees.

The New Jersey Assembly had adopted its first resolution in 1882 "demanding protection for the oppressed Jews of Russia." This reminder appeared in the Vineland *Journal* along with later protests from eminent world figures, such as Gladstone, who expressed his "horror at the cruelties of the Russian Government toward the Jews." Tolstoy's statement on the Kishinev massacre was also reprinted: "My relation to the Jews can only be as that to brothers whom I love . . . . [Horror and pity] mingled with perplexity at the bestiality of the so-called educated people who instigated the mob . . . the government, with its foolish, fanatical priesthood and gang of robber officials . . . hesitating at no atrocity. . . . The Kishinev crime was a consequence of preaching lies and violence which the government carries on with such stubborn energy."

In response to the new Kishinev pogrom, Philadelphians held three protest meetings, while at a Baltimore meeting three thousand people heard, among other things, a statement from Cardinal Gibbons; reprinted verbatim in the *Journal,* it expressed his "abhorrence at the massacres that have carried to their graves gray hair and innocent childhood." In Atlantic City, too, Jewish Chautauquans met in protest and listened as the oppression of Russian Jews was dramatically depicted by former immigration commissioner John B. Weber, who headed a congressional committee studying causes of mass migration to the United States. (Brandes, Joseph. *Immigrants to Freedom.)*

American Students Demonstrate for Soviet Jewry *(text, page 80)*

The Soviet Union continues to oppress Eastern European Jews today. Here is a report of how American students are working to rally public opinion on behalf of Soviet Jewry and to show the world that Jews are all part of one people.

More than 500 Yeshiva high school students gathered at the Isaiah Wall across from the United Nations to mark the eighth night of Chanukah with prayers in solidarity with Soviet Jewry. Following the afternoon prayer service, Michael Berl, music teacher at Ramaz, led the students in traditional holiday songs.

Rabbi Haskel Lookstein, principal of the Ramaz School and organizer of the event, described his recent experiences in the Soviet Union. A recent emigre from Riga, Mrs. Bella Ulman, then urged those present to speak out on behalf of her son, Misha, and others who are denied permission to go to Israel. The lighting of a large menorah ended the vigil.

Among the participants were students of the Frisch School, Hebrew Academy of Nassau County, Hillel School and Ramaz. The program was coordinated by the G.N.Y.C.S.J. *(Update.* The Greater New York Conference on Soviet Jewry, January, 1973.)

The Dearborn Independent *(text, page 81)*

In the 1920's, Henry Ford's newspaper, *The Dearborn Independent*, published a long series of deceptive articles about a secret "Jewish plot" to take over the world. In the selection below, Ford's paper tries to prove that the Hebrew religious hymn, *Eli, Eli,* is really anti-Christian propaganda being spread by a secret Jewish organization known as the "Kehilla." This "secret organization" was, of course, a total fabrication by the author of the articles.

Now, as to the Jewish religious hymn which is being sung "by request" throughout the country: the story of it is soon told.

The name of the hymn is "Eli, Eli"; its base is the first verse of the Twenty-second Psalm, known best in Christian countries as the Cry of Christ on the Cross.

It is being used by Jewish vaudeville managers as their contribution to the pro-Jewish campaign which the Jew-controlled theater is flinging into the faces of the public, from stage and motion picture screen. It is an incantation designed to inflame the lower classes of Jews against the people, and intensify the racial consciousness of those hordes of Eastern Jews who have flocked here.

At the instigation of the New York Kehillah, "Eli, Eli" has for a long time been sung at the ordinary run of performances in vaudeville and motion picture houses, and the notice "By Request" is usually a bald lie. It should be "By Order." The "request" is from Jewish headquarters which has ordered the speeding up of Jewish propaganda. The situation of the theater now is that American audiences are paying at the box office for the privilege of hearing Jews advertise the things they want non-Jews to think about them.

This Yiddish chant is the rallying cry of race hatred which is being spread abroad by orders of the Jewish leaders.

"Eli, Eli" is not a religious hymn! It is a racial war cry. In the low cafes of New York, where Bolshevik Jews hang out, "Eli, Eli" is their song. It is the Marseillaise of Jewish solidarity. It has become the fanatical chant of all Jewish Bolshevik clubs; it is constantly heard in Jewish coffee houses and cabarets where emotional Russian and Polish Jews—all enemies to all government—shout the words amid torrential excitement. When you see the hymn in point you are utterly puzzled to understand the excitement it rouses.

And this rallying cry has now been obtruded into the midst of the theatrical world.

(The International Jew: A Selection of Articles from the Dearborn Independent. Dearborn: The Dearborn Publishing Co., 1921.)

A Jew in the Army (text, page 84)

Leon Blum was a private in the U.S. army during World War Two. In this letter to his parents he speaks as both a Jew and an American. As a Jew he is outraged at what the Nazis are doing to his own people, and as an American he is angry that men are persecuting their fellow men.

England

Dear Mom:

You asked me to write about what the Jewish boys are doing for this army. I wish I could write better and really express myself because there is an awful lot to tell. . . .

The Jewish boys here are just what you would expect. They like their fun and they can do their work just as well as any other group of men. The boys here take all kinds of hardships . . . with a smile and a joke. But anyone can see that underneath this lightheartedness is a certain forcefulness of purpose. The Jew has been "kicked around" for many centuries in many countries, but his faith is still strong and he can fight for his rights and decencies. The boys here know just what has been going on in Europe. They know of the persecution and terrors that their brother Jews have been going through . . . The American Jew stands ready to fight to the death for the rights of all men regardless of their religion or color, all over the world . . . The American Jew stands ready and extends his helping hand to whoever needs it. It is this generosity and sincerity of purpose that has always been a part of the

Jewish culture that keeps the Jewish faith alive and vibrant through the centuries.

You don't ever have to worry about the outcome of this war, the victory will be ours, and whatever part the Jew plays in the peace it will be for the equality and rights of all men over the earth.

Your son,
Leon

(Rontch, Isaac, ed. *Jewish Youth at War*.)

An American Jew Reacts to the Holocaust (text, page 84)

Rabbi Richard Rubenstein, a modern American theologian, believes that the destruction of six million Jews during World War Two created a major upheaval in Jewish thinking today. Here are some of his feelings about the Holocaust.

We cannot restore the religious world which preceded [the six million's] demise, nor can we ignore the fact that the catastrophe has had and will continue to have an extraordinary influence on Jewish life. Although Jewish history is replete with disaster, none has been so radical in its total import as the holocaust. Our images of God, man, and the moral order have been permanently impaired. No Jewish theology will possess even a remote degree of relevance to contemporary Jewish life if it ignores the question of God and the death camps. That is *the question* for Jewish theology in our times. Regrettably most attempts at formulating a Jewish theology since World War II seem to have been written as if the two decisive events of our time for Jews, the death camps and the birth of Israel, had not taken place.

A religious community has some resemblance to a living organism. It is impossible savagely to rip out half of its substance without drastically affecting the surviving remnant. The first reaction to such a wounding must be shock and numbness. I do not believe the period of shock has entirely spent itself. It is only now that a tentative attempt can be made to assess the religious meaning of the events. (Rubenstein, Richard. *After Auschwitz*. New York: Bobbs-Merrill Co., Inc., 1966.)

Israel

Jewish Nationhood in America (text, page 15)

In his book *If I Forget Thee O Jerusalem*, Robert Silverberg compares Jewishness in America with Jewishness in Israel. As Americans, we naturally feel a loyalty to the United States; but as Jews, we also feel an attachment to Israel. Our concern for the Jewish State in Israel demonstrates our dual identity as both Jews and Americans.

The tourist in Israel is startled by the *Jewishness* of it all. On my first night in Tel Aviv I felt . . . amazement . . . as I saw Hebrew signs on every storefront, Hebrew letters on traffic signals, Hebrew menus posted outside every restaurant. It seemed incredible to me that everyone hurrying across the street at one busy intersection should be Jewish, and the children tossing a ball should cry out to one another in Hebrew.

In the United States . . . Jews learn not to make themselves too conspicuous; it is a reflex, an exaggerated reaction to the fear of anti-Semitism, perhaps. A Jew remembers that he is Jewish, and therefore somehow different from most of the other people on the street. He knows that these strangers, wearing their crucifixes or thinking about last Sunday's church service . . . share neither his childhood background nor, probably, his opinions on a thousand questions. In the United States, the Jew can remember meeting friendly, wholly sympathetic Gentiles who questioned him about his beliefs . . . as though he were a Martian.

In Israel, where Jewishness is universal, the American Jewish tourist . . . does not need to feel like an alien. In Tel Aviv it is the *goy* who is the alien. The Jew does not have to make, here, the little explanations that he was always making in the United States. ("A Jew doesn't take his hat *off* when he enters an important place. He puts his hat *on*." "The Jewish Sabbath is Saturday, not Sunday. Actually, it starts on Friday at sundown." "There isn't really a priesthood in Judaism any more. A rabbi is more of a community leader than a priest.") In Israel everybody knows all that—knows it a good deal better than he does himself. (Silverberg, Robert. *If I Forget Thee, O Jerusalem.* New York: Wm. Morrow & Co., 1970.)

Israel Changes the Jew's Image (text, page 80)

In their poll of American Jewish attitudes, Marshall Sklare, Joseph Greenblum, and Benjamin Ringer posed this question: "Do you think the existence of the State of Israel has had any effect on the status and security of American Jews?" Here are the results of their survey.

Among the majority who consider Israel a boon rather than a threat, the favorite arguments were that Israel was helping to strengthen the self-awareness and the religious and ethnic ties of Jews in this country or, especially, to improve gentiles' attitudes toward Jews. Israel, it was said, had created a new image of the Jew as fighter and frontiersman; gentiles admired what the Israelis did; Israel showed the non-Jewish community that Jews could "stand up and fight—that the Jew is a *man*, not just a merchant."

An engineer who believed that Israel's image counteracted anti-Semitic sterotyping summed it up with the observation: "The American Jew has acquired more status because Jewish people showed themselves to be pioneers, soldiers, farmers—things that people didn't know they could do. Israel shows they have *guts*. And now gentiles take a different look at their Jewish neighbors." (Sklare, Greenblum, Ringer. *Not Quite at Home.*)

The Six-Day War (text, page 85)

The establishment of a Jewish state in Israel greatly enhanced the self-esteem of American Jews. As we can see from this passage, Israel's dramatic fight for survival in 1967 had a great impact on the solidarity of the Jewish people.

On Monday morning, June 5, 1967, I was awakened as usual by the sound of my radio-clock, automatically turning itself on to deliver the 8 A.M. news. The news that morning was grim. "War has broken out in the Near East," the announcer said. "Aircraft of Egypt, Jordan, Syria, and Iraq have bombed Israel. Radio Cairo reports that Tel Aviv is in flames and an oil refinery near Haifa has been destroyed. Algeria, Morocco, Tunisia, the Sudan, Kuwait, Yemen, Lebanon, and Saudi Arabia have announced declarations of war against Israel. There has been no word as yet from the Israeli government on conditions there."

Scarcely awake yet, I felt a sudden chill of terror. . . . I pictured waves of Arab planes streaking in from the Mediterranean or from the desert and smashing, in a few hours, what had taken so long to build. I saw the Russian-built tanks of Egypt rolling through the shattered streets of Tel Aviv . . . And I felt a sense of personal anguish and loss, as though the enemy were marching up my own street toward the comfortable house where I lay still abed.

Even in that moment of fear and despair, I paused to wonder at my own presumptuousness. By what right did I allow myself the luxury of these emotions? What, after all, did Israel mean to me, that I should be so deeply concerned? . . . Up to that time I had never visited the place, never contributed a penny toward its development, never recognized in myself any special involvement with its fortunes. As a secularized New York Jew . . . I certainly could claim no mystic religious bond with the land of the Bible. It was reasonable for me to react to the Arab attack as I would to any act of violence, to any suppression of freedom, to any destruction . . . Yet I trembled for Israel, and mourned for her devastated cities, in a way that was entirely different in depth from my response to [other world tragedies]. . . . in that first instant it seemed to me that by attacking Israel, the Arabs had attacked some extension of myself. And I was baffled by the source of that powerful emotion. . . .

As the details of [Israel's] glorious victory emerged, I felt anguish give way to wonder, and then to a pride in Israel's victory that was totally unearned . . . How splendidly "we" had fought, I told myself; how fine it was that "we" had once again foiled the villainous Arabs. *We!* I, no Zionist, hardly even a Jew except by birth, was [now] identifying myself with the Israeli warriors. (Silverberg, Robert. *If I Forget Thee, O Jerusalem.*)

INDEX